The
Practical
Vegetable
Gardener

The Practical Vegetable Gardener

by John Philip Baumgardt

New York   London   Tokyo

Standard Book Number: 0–8256–3094–0
Library of Congress Catalog Card Number: 77–088751

In Great Britain: Book Sales Ltd., 78 Newman Street, London W1.

In Canada: Gage Trade Publishing, P.O. Box 5000, 164 Commander Blvd.,
Agincourt, Ontario M1S 3C7.

In Japan: Music Sales Corporation, 4–26–22 Jingumae, Shibuya-Ku,
Tokyo 150.

Cover illustration by Jane Clark.
Book and cover design by Iris Weinstein.

Contents

Introduction   9

Planning Your Garden   11

The best location for a vegetable garden   13

Vegetables suitable for backyard growing   15

Soil preparation and management   17

Sowing seeds and setting plants   24

Summer cultivation and summer mulching   26

How to plan a seasonal crop rotation   27

A design for a small, long-season garden   30

Vegetables from A to Z   35

Fertilizers for vegetables   172

Composts and manures for vegetables   176

Growing vegetables in containers   180

Glossary   186

Quick Reference Chart   188

Index   189

Introduction

Everyone can grow a few vegetables. Property owners are lucky because they can raise anything from a small patch of a few vegetable favorites to a sizable kitchen garden capable of supplying almost all the vegetables the family needs throughout the entire year.

But even apartment dwellers can raise a few edibles on the balcony, patio, or windowsill. Parsley in a pot is very decorative, and is also a fine source of garnish, flavor, and vitamins. The new small-sized tomato plants, such as 'Patio', grow well and produce great fruit in a pot. (I would recommend finding seed of the currant tomato, *Lycopersicon pimpinellifolium,* and growing it in a hanging basket.) I have even seen fine bush squash growing in soil-filled bushel baskets on terraces and balconies.

As I said, everybody can have a vegetable garden. It pays, any way you look at it.

Gardening is a productive sort of recreation. As you putter about the property you are building the sort of environment that suits you best. And, incidentally, your property value goes up as your creative design develops. There alone is a combination of aesthetic and financial gain.

Your gardens provide plants and flowers for the house. The vegetable garden, especially, furnishes far better produce than the supermarket provides. And, there are those special delicacies often unobtainable in most stores—fresh-picked snow peas, baby carrots, summer squash with fresh blossoms still attached.

While increased costs of fertilizers, composts, and seeds may raise the cost of home-produced garden vegetables, dollar for dollar, the home produce is far superior. You are gaining quality.

Planning
Your Garden

There are dozens of ways to approach the design and size of a vegetable garden. Take into consideration your method of cultivation, the amount of space and time you wish to allot to vegetable gardening, and the yields of vegetables you expect to harvest.

Let's consider soil preparation and cultivation. If you plan to go mechanical, using the smallest garden tractor-type machine, you ought to think of a garden with a long axis of at least 50 feet, otherwise the tractor cannot maneuver efficiently. Beyond the garden area, the tractor needs at least 15 feet at each end on which to turn. A rotary tiller can operate in less space but it also needs some amount of free run in the garden and a turning area of grass or walkway. The garden should be a minimum of 30 feet long, and six or eight feet is required to turn a worthwhile tiller. Before planning on tractors or tillers, read the section on Soil Preparation and Management. It may present some views you'll need to consider when making your decisions. There is the possibility of spading the garden. This is the very best sort of soil preparation. It produces the best crops, gives *you* the best exercise, and requires no extra turn-around space.

A Chicago friend of mine operates a beautiful vegetable garden. There is a long axis of fine lawn about 15 feet wide (recently a five-foot-wide brick walk was put down the middle of this) and a 15-foot panel of fine lawn runs the breadth of the garden entrance. On each side of the long walk are three 15- × 20-foot vegetable plots separated from one another by five-foot-wide grass paths. A fruit and flower border, six feet wide, surrounds the entire design. The six beds are hand-spaded as needed. Because they are separate, it is easy to arrange various crop rotations, spacings, and planting times. This garden, with 1,800 square feet of growing area, more than feeds a family of four, fills their freezer for the winter, and yields excess vegetables to give to friends.

If you never have gardened before, I suggest that you confine your efforts the first year to a single small plot that is 15 feet wide and 20 to 25 feet long. You will have to forego space-demanding crops such as sweet corn, vining squashes, and okra, but you will be able to produce remarkable quantities of the smaller vegetables such as peas, beans, lettuces, radishes, carrots, beets, kohlrabi, tomatoes, peppers, a few bush squashes, and even a few of the rather widespread members of the cabbage family. Such a plot, managed to the utmost, could easily keep you busy and supply most of your fresh produce for summer eating. The maintenance time should not run more than two hours each week for a skilled gardener, twice that for a beginner.

To summarize, if you plan to machine-operate your garden, plan to make it big because the rows have to be wide apart, and make it in one long piece for farm-like efficiency. If you are going to hand-operate the garden, it can be much smaller because rows will be closer. The minimum space ought to be 150 square feet for each member of the family for most efficient operation, and the maximum is up to you. But by all means, start small. You can add more garden next year. It seems easy to spade up or to plow an extensive area in the spring and to plant a sizable area to crops. But then the weeds begin to grow and that vast area has to be tilled frequently, rows have to be hand-weeded and hand-thinned, and it all becomes a laborious effort. Take on only what you can manage comfortably; make your first garden smallish. You always can work up more soil for a fall garden.

The best location for a vegetable garden

We city dwellers seem to have to locate our vegetable gardens where they least interfere with the general landscaping scheme. This sometimes is good, sometimes unfortunate. Let's consider the vegetable plants' requirements—conditions for optimum growth—and then take a look at possible adaptations.

Drainage is important. Almost without exception, vegetables have been developed over the years to grow on well-drained soil. Just because property may slope so that rainfall runs off quickly does not mean that the soil is particularly well drained. Never locate a vegetable garden at the bottom of a slope or even toward the lower part of a slope. It should be placed toward the top. If your soil is tight and compact, you may have to work it deeply (as described in the Soil Preparation section) to bring it into high productivity.

Full sun is important. Commercial vegetables are produced in open fields and the modern vegetable strains are bred to grow in a fully open exposure. The plants do poorly in shade. You may grow some rather spindly plants in the lee of the house or where a large tree shades them for part of the day, but they never will be as productive or healthy as they would be if grown in the open.

There is another aspect of growing a garden near trees and shrubs. The roots of these woody species will grow into your well-worked, fertile vegetable patch and rob the vegetables of needed minerals and water. The good vegetable garden always is far enough away from trees and shrubs that roots cannot encroach.

Convenience fits into the picture, but not too strongly. While it is handy to have the vegetable patch close to the hose bib, at the kitchen door, not too far from the toolshed, or near the driveway for delivery of manures and other heavy materials, these are conveniences to forego if the garden can be sited in a better drained, sunnier spot. In many cases the victory gardens of World War II were on public land two or three miles from people's dwellings. There was no gas to drive to the garden, but vegetable lovers loaded up their tools, watering cans, and water in junior's red wagon and trundled off each evening to garden. A friend in Copenhagen whose government-operated allotment garden is nearly six miles from his apartment tells me that half the fun of gardening is the evening bicycle ride (with the missus on her bike, too) to the community allotments. He is 66 years old! Don't let the urge for convenience lead you to locate the garden where growing conditions are less than good.

Have you ever noticed that commercial greenhouses stretch north and south, seldom east and west? Have you noticed that commercial truck gardeners usually run their rows north and south? There is a good reason for this polarity. The sun rises in the east, swings overhead, tending toward a southerly path through much of the year, and sets in the west. Plant rows running north and south receive about an equal exposure of sunlight during the day. If rows run east and west, the south side of the row gets most of the sunlight and the north side gets very little. This can make a real difference with plants bred for full-light exposure. By all means, try to plan your garden so rows can run north and south.

To summarize, locate your garden in the open, with full sun, and away from the invading roots of trees and shrubs. Locate it where vertical soil drainage is good and where runoff is minimal (on as level a site as you have). Where possible, if the above criteria are met, locate the garden so it is handy to the house, the driveway, the toolshed, and the hose bib.

Vegetables suitable for backyard growing

Within limitations of weather and soil, the vegetables in your garden will be determined by your taste and available space. I know one salad enthusiast who fills every inch of her ground with ingredients for the salad bowl; she grows half a dozen kinds of lettuces and radishes as well as scallions, shallots, chives, cherry tomatoes, lovage, cucumbers, beets, and carrots, all to be eaten raw. Her efforts with cauliflower and celery have failed to date but she still is trying. A gentleman friend loves sweet corn. He grows a few early peas and lettuce, but his heart is not in these. Beginning in April, he sows four short rows of sweet corn every two weeks and by early July he is eating corn-on-the-cob which continues into October. In your garden, grow what you like to eat. There is nothing you have to grow. But don't cheat yourself of the taste pleasure of an unfamiliar vegetable or something strange. Look up the detailed cultural instructions of these "new" vegetables and have a go at them.

Early in the game you will learn that some vegetables grow best in cool weather, others thrive only in the heat of summer. To get the most of your garden, plan to grow cool-weather crops in early spring and through the fall months, and grow the hot-weather plants in summer. (*See* pages 31 – 33). I bring this up now to save you some disappointments. If you were to plant green beans in March or lettuce in July, probably you would not harvest a crop of either.

Some of the easiest and most productive vegetables for the home garden are:

Green beans, Carrots, Lettuce, Beets, Sweet corn, Onions, Cabbage, Kohlrabi, Peas, Sweet peppers, Swiss chard, Radishes, Spinach, Summer squash, Tomatoes, Turnips.

If you grow a respectable crop of each of these, say, just what a seed packet would produce (less in the case of cabbage, peppers, and tomatoes), probably you will halve your grocery bill for the summer and there will be extra vegetables for the neighbors or for the freezer.

Perhaps you have plenty of space and time. In that case, you can add almost any vegetable you wish to grow that will grow well in your area. You may want to branch out into:

> **Shell beans, Broccoli, *Cauliflower, Field beans, Brussels sprouts, *Celeriac, Lima beans, Savoy cabbage, *Celery, *Broad beans, Chinese cabbage, *Chicory, *Collards, Kale, Pumpkins, Cucumbers, Leeks, Winter squash, *Eggplant, Mustard, *Rutabagas, Endive, Parsnips, Fennel, Hot peppers.**

And still there are more kinds of vegetables: asparagus, cardoons, garlic, Jerusalem artichoke, garden cress, herbs of many kinds, and more. You may make up your own list from all of these suggested sorts. Always bear in mind space, soil, growing conditions and exposure. Space-demanding crops such as Savoy cabbage, sweet corn, sprawling squashes, pumpkins, and the like take up too much space for the average city garden. Parsnips are easy and very good eating but they do take up an entire row of the garden from spring through summer and into the late fall. Some vegetables are in the second list because people just do not know them well enough. I could recommend most of them. But if you were to grow a great bed of Florence fennel and then not know how to cope with it in the kitchen or if it turned out that you disliked it, what then? Stick to vegetables you really enjoy and try just one or two of the stranger ones each year until your garden is big enough to allow experimental crops without sacrificing vegetables you really use and enjoy.

---

*These vegetables are difficult for one reason or another. Eggplants go buggy, cauliflower is very demanding with regard to soil and weather, chicory is tricky to handle if you want perfect Witloof shoots, and so on. A beginner is apt to get into difficulty with any of these.

Soil preparation and management

The best investment you can make in time and effort in the vegetable garden is thorough soil preparation. The very finest seeds available will not make productive plants in poorly worked soil. No amount of expensive fertilizer will bring out succulent, vigorous vegetable plants from poorly prepared soil. Here we can learn a lesson from the British gardeners. They really do a job of working their soil. For the British, gardening begins and ends with soil management. As a result, their ornamentals and vegetables grow magnificently. Several aspects of soil management must be considered.

Topsoil

A gardener grows plants in topsoil. Topsoil is soil that is less compact than subsoil, so air can diffuse down to supply oxygen to the roots and the drainage is fast. Topsoil usually contains a fairly high percentage of humus, that is, organic residues originating from decayed leaves, stems, and roots of plants, from soil additives such as compost and peat, or even from sawdust, ground corn cobs, rice or buckwheat hulls, or other once-living (organic) debris. This organic fraction of the soil is important. Due to its spongy nature it holds moisture that is necessary for plant roots, while it separates the soil mineral particles which tend to settle too tightly together, preventing good drainage and aeration. As humus breaks down, humic acids modify the soil texture beneficially. Some organic gardeners feel that by adding manures and composts to the soil all the nutrients that the soil needs to carry a strong crop are supplied. Unless we are talking about adding 40 pounds or more of fresh barnyard manure per square yard each year, this is nearly impossible. Organic residues are relatively low in readily available nutrients. One thousand pounds of barnyard manure has about the same nutritional value as a 100-pound sack of 5–10–5 fertilizer. The real advantage of using organic materials is their beneficial effect on soil texture. These residues convert subsoil to topsoil. They do not fertilize plants, but modify the soil so the plants grow very well—if enough fertilizer is added.

Topsoil, then, should be loose, fast-draining, well-aerated soil high in organic residues, which supports good plant growth. The deeper the topsoil layer, the deeper plant roots penetrate, and the more resistant plants become to above-ground environmental stress conditions. It is the gardener's business to continuously improve and deepen the topsoil.

Fertilizers

When we take garden produce into the house to eat, we want the nutrition, the vitamins, minerals, and food value they contain. While the plants manufacture part of these through photosynthesis, the remainder come from the soil. Thus, each successive crop impoverishes the soil. To grow the biggest and best vegetables, we have to fertilize each crop as it begins, while it is growing and, in a few cases, as it matures. An interesting sidelight is the fact that often subsoil is relatively rich in plant nutrients but these cannot be utilized by the plants as their roots cannot penetrate the airless, dense mineral layers.

Your job, then, is to practice a year-round program of soil management which preserves a soil fertility level suitable for each species you grow. Plant nutrients may be divided into two groups: those used in relatively large amounts; and those essential to normal plant growth which are required only in the minutest quality, either a deficiency or an overdose being detrimental. Read the sections on Fertilizers (page 172) and Composts (page 176) for technical details. For now, it suffices to point out that the minerals most used up by plants are nitrogen (N), phosphorus (P), and potassium (K). On every bag of fertilizer there are three numbers, for example, 5–10–5 or 10–6–4. The first number represents the amount of nitrogen; the second, phosphorus; the third, potassium (the latter two in oxidized form). The three numbers are referred to as the NPK ratio and, using the first example, it tells us that the bag contains, per 100 pounds, 5 pounds of nitrogen, 10 pounds of phosphoric acid, and 5 pounds of potassium oxide (potash)—or other percentages as the numbers indicate.

Keep in mind that different plants grow best when fertilized in different ways. Spend the winter months reading the specific details for fertilizing each vegetable crop. Also, refer to the soil improvement and crop rotation chart (page 28), which shows how various portions of the garden may be treated each year so specific crops can be fitted to soil prepared optimally for them.

Drainage

Soil right at the surface may be tight, impervious to air and water, and unsuitable for plant growth, but unless water is seeping up from below usually it is possible in a year or two to develop a foot or so of topsoil, and more in subsequent years. There is a simple way to check on vertical drainage in your garden soil: Take a spade to the proposed garden site and dig a hole, laying the soil layers aside *unmixed* so you can study the soil variation as you dig deeper. The relatively loose, upper layer where sod or weed roots penetrate is topsoil. It may vary from a few inches to several feet in depth. If it is very shallow you have a real job facing you. If it is reasonably deep your job is less involved. What about the stuff underlying the topsoil? Is it very tight and hard, or is it reasonably permeable? Tight, hard subsoil will act just like the bottom of the bathtub. No matter how well drained the topsoil above, water will collect when it hits the sub-soil layer, and during a wet spell it will back up into the topsoil and drown plant roots. To check on the porosity of your subsoil, dig three or four holes in the proposed garden site (they should not be more than 10 feet apart in recently graded and developed soil, 20 feet apart in undisturbed soils). The holes should be the width of a spade or sharpshooter, and about 18 inches deep. This is a project to carry out in mid-spring or mid-fall when it is rainy, but wait until the soil is just moderately damp, say, two or three days after the last good rain. Fill each hole up to the top with water. Observe how long it takes to soak away; if the water is gone in two hours or less, your deep drainage is good, you have no drainage problem. If it takes up to four hours, you need to do some double-digging or trenching. If the water remains for longer than four hours, you absolutely have to do something about vertical drainage; you'll have to do some deep digging, install a tile field, or something else.

Methods of Turning Soil

Before a crop can be planted it is necessary to turn the topsoil, loosening it so seed drills may be opened, and to incorporate composts, manures, and fertilizers. One method is to dig up the soil with a spade and turn it over by hand—this is called *spading*. Another method is to pull a curved blade through it, a blade that cuts the soil and rolls it over into an adjacent furrow, also inverting the soil, as in spading. This is called *plowing*. Both spading and plowing aim to bury soil which was on top and move to the surface soil which was buried. Good spading and good plowing enable us to incorporate soil-texture-improving substances such as manures, leaf molds, composts, and other organic residues, as well as fertilizers and limes, and it should be done in such a way that the normal structure of the soil is not excessively disturbed. This is an important point: good gardening and agricultural soils have a "grain" somewhat analogous to the grain of wood. If the soil is abused—worked when wet, excessively stirred, subjected to compaction by heavy equipment—the grain may be modified or destroyed, which changes aeration and drainage and negatively affects plant root growth.

A third method sometimes used to prepare soil is with a *rotary tiller*. Advertising leads us to believe that we can buy a rotary cultivator, rush out and stir the soil to a depth of a few inches, plant a crop, and expect miracles. The miracle is that anything at all grows under such a program. Rotary tillers are suitable for lightly cultivating soil which already has been properly turned either by hand or by mechanical means. Except in the loosest of soils, rotary cultivators are worthless for doing the primary job of turning soil, and where they do manage to dig in, they overlick the soil to an overaerated condition. This sounds as if I disapprove of tillers. Not so. I own two of them, and use them for cultivating throughout the summer and to turn under freshly shredded cornstalks and similar debris. But I never would use a tiller to prepare the soil in the spring. I must also say that I never have had any satisfaction with a tiller with the rotary cultivator in front. In my experience, manhandling one of these front-end tillers is akin to wrestling an elephant, and the machines merely skip over the surface of the ground. I would never consider anything but a tiller with the tines mounted behind the wheels, and I want a good, heavy machine, capable of properly penetrating the soil. For a city garden, I think power machines, either plows or tillers, are expensive, pointless luxuries. For anything less than a 2,000-square-foot garden all you need is a good digging spade and a few cultivating tools.

Spading the Garden

Let's proceed, using two examples. In the first case, your soil is well drained and with a reasonable depth of topsoil. In the second instance drainage is not too good and the topsoil is shallow. Obviously, the two conditions will be handled differently. The first calls for nothing more than simple spading, at least until you become a really dedicated gardener. But in the second case we will have to do some deep digging to create good topsoil.

When the soil drains well and there is a reasonably good

layer of topsoil, working up ground for the vegetable garden is not a great chore. There are several steps; clearing away any plant material present—sod, weeds, and so on; providing for the addition of composts, manures, fertilizers, and lime (if needed); and the actual business of sticking the spade into the earth, hoisting out a chunk, and putting it back in a time-honored way.

Bear in mind that the garden is spaded with a spade, not with a turning fork. Lacking a garden spade you can use a shiny bladed, razor-edged, roundnosed shovel, but the results will not be as good.

The first step in spading is to clear the surface of plant growth. With your spade blade held nearly parallel to the ground, sharp edge forward, shave off the plants just below the soil line. This is good material for the compost pile, or you can windrow it along the edge of the garden to be strewn on the bottom of your digging trench to provide deep humus in the bed.

Next, top-dress the stripped soil with a layer of compost, barnyard manure, or other organic debris that is relatively decayed. Now digging can proceed.

At one end of the garden, mark off a two-foot-wide area the width of the garden. Lift the soil from this area and wheelbarrow it to the far end of the garden and deposit it on the grass, clear of the garden area. Now you have an open trench the width of the garden, two feet wide, the depth of a spade blade (spit). Mark off the next two-foot area. Scatter the manure or comost from this area onto the bottom of the first trench. At the edge of the garden at one end of the second area, insert the spade blade vertically and pull it out; move over the width of the spade blade and make a similar vertical cut; with the spade blade parallel to the face of the trench, insert the spade between the two cuts and lift out the spit of soil, and invert it as you place it into the first trench. Make your next cut adjacent to the second one, and so proceed to cut free, lift out, invert, and replace chunks of soil. This is real spading. It sounds complicated and there are several variations to the technique, but any of them is quite simple once you get the idea and begin digging. As you spade back and forth across the garden, you are continuously maintaining a trench in which to work and are scraping up the top-dressing to be placed below the turned soil. (A real purist scrapes up the top-dressing and scatters it along the face of each row of turned spits before proceeding to the next row of spading and so distributes the organic matter from the top to the bottom of the turned soil.) When you reach the final two feet of the garden you will have run out of soil, so you use the soil (resting on the grass) from that first trench to fill in this area. Soil properly spaded is even (level), uniform in surface texture, and coarse appearing. Ideally, soil is spaded in the fall, allowed to fallow over winter so frost can work into the clods, and in the spring sections are lightly forked and worked down to prepare the soil for planting seeds.

Double-Digging to Improve Soil Depth and Drainage

Let's assume that you are stuck with poorly drained soil with shallow topsoil. This calls for deeper work so the soil is loosened and improved to a greater depth; the simplest way is a technique called double-digging. Start as above, with an open two-foot-wide trench at one end of the garden. Dress the bottom of the trench with as thick a layer of barnyard manure or enriched compost as you can; a two-inch layer is all right, more is better. With a spading fork, turn the soil in the bottom of the trench in place, mixing the organic matter through the subsoil as you go. The effect of loosening this lower spit of soil is aeration and improved drainage; as the organic matter is digested away by soil microorganisms, subsoil becomes topsoil, so your garden eventually will have fertile topsoil some 20 to 26 inches deep, depending on the blade lengths of your spade and fork.

The best procedure is to double-dig one-third of the garden every year (spade the rest) so that over a three-year period all of the soil is deeply worked and built up with organic residues and, if needed, with fertilizer amendments. In my garden the subsoil is lacking in calcium and is overly acidic. To correct this, agricultural limestone is dressed over the floor of each trench (with the composts and manures) and is then turned in deeply, as is a light dressing of superphosphate to make up for the shortage indicated by a soil test. The County Agent always is amazed when I take in subsoil samples—he has never heard of deep cultivation!

Plowing and Rotary Tilling

Most machines available will not turn soil to a depth of more than six or eight inches, and some gardeners seem to be satisfied with the results they get from shallow gardening. A small tractor plow, properly used, gives results vaguely similar to simple spading. Clear the soil so the blade can cut efficiently; top-dress the garden with a generous layer of manure, compost, leaf mold or other organic material. Then plow, working as deeply as possible, at a speed which wall cause the soil to roll over as it leaves the plow. A garden that is plowed in the fall, left fallow over winter, and worked up for planting in spring will produce quite good vegetable crops.

Do not work your soil in the fall with a rotary cultivator. These machines churn up the soil and break down the normal texture ("overlicking" is the technical term) and such "milled" soil will settle down and compact tightly over winter. Rather, clear off the garden and run all of the plant debris through a hot compost to destroy insects and diseases. Some of these will over-winter in the undisturbed soil, but there is no way to get around that. In spring, when you are ready to plant, dress the soil generously with finished compost or old barnyard manure, and such fertilizers and lime as the crop indicates; set the tiller to operate as deeply *and as slowly* as possible, and work over the soil just one time. Reworking overaerates the soil, powdering it so the first heavy rain (and your feet as you plant and cultivate) will pack it down into an impervious hardness.

Sowing seeds and setting plants

Not every crop is planted at the same time. In very early spring, seeds of the frost-tolerant vegetables are planted: lettuces, spinach, radishes, peas, broad beans, and the like. You may choose to plant a few onion sets or plants. A little later on beet, carrot, leek, parsnip, and similar cold-germinating seeds go in and plants of cauliflower, cabbage, broccoli, and brussels sprouts are set. Finally, when the soil is warm, it is time for beans, squash, peppers, tomatoes, sweet corn, okra, eggplant, and other hot-weather sorts. Make it a practice to work up just as much soil as you need at a time, leaving the remainder rough (if a crop of weeds appears you will have to work it down and cultivate shallowly from time to time).

It is a good idea to make up a chart of your entire garden, showing the spacing for rows of various crops (as recommended on seed packets or in the A to Z section of this book). This enables you to account for all the vegetables you wish to grow in the space you have, and to lay out follow-up crops so the entire garden is in production throughout the length of the growing season. The alphabetical listing of vegetables in this book will help you with spacings, seed depth, germination, crop duration (time to maturity), and so on.

To open drills (the furrows for sowing seeds), set stakes at both ends of the row and stretch a cord between them. Walk alongside this line using a sharp hoe to pull out the soil to make a drill of appropriate depth. This is called "drawing open a drill." The soil from the drill should be placed neatly and uniformly to *one* side of the trench. Usually soil is moist enough so seed may be sown directly. During summer months, however, it is often necessary to moisten powder-dry soil for successful germination. With a sprinkling can (open spout) or a hose, gently flood the bottom of the drill; take care not to erode the sides. Then sow the seeds on the mud and pull the dry soil in on them. The water will seep upwards by capillarity to dampen both seeds and the overlying soil. *Do not* add water on top of the covered seeds, as the soil will then crust, making germination impossible.

In a few cases you will find recommendations to place fertilizer under the seed. *Seed must never be in direct contact with fertilizers or manures*. Make an extra-deep drill, then scatter the fertilizer on the bottom. Cover with at least an inch of soil and gently firm this by patting with the back of a rake; then sow seed as usual.

To cover seed (usually to a depth of two to four times its thickness as it lies in the drill): with a steel rake or small hoe, pull soil taken from the drill over the seed; at first work slowly and carefully until you develop a good technique. For uniform germination the seed must be covered evenly. Next, walk the length of the row, patting down the soil with the back of the steel rake. Some gardeners prefer to walk, toe to heel, down the rows of large seeds, such as beans and sweet corn. Finally, if you want your garden to look like a fine British kitchen garden, pull the rake *lightly* down the row and rake between rows where you have walked so the final appearance is of loose, undisturbed soil. Such a surface takes in rain uniformly and tiny weed seedlings show up well. When those weeds do appear, catch them as early as possible, when a simple, shallow raking will uproot them for the sun to destroy.

By all means, keep your soil and seeded rows weed-free. After the garden has been in weed-free cultivation for a few years all the seeds lying dormant in the soil will have sprouted and weeding will be a relatively easy proposition. But in a new garden, and in a garden that is allowed to go weedy each year, every few days brings on a new crop of weeds. Crawl (or squat) along the row and hand-weed your seedlings; at the same time you can thin them to recommended spacings. Rake or cultivate between rows to keep down weeds.

Most crops require an occasional side-dressing of fertilizer as they develop. Follow the instructions for using fertilizer carefully in order to achieve top-quality yields. Keep in mind that some plants do not tolerate additional fertilizers, so be sure to check the recommended amounts for each kind of plant.

As soon as a crop is harvested, clear away the residues, if any. Compost this debris, then dress the soil with the compost and fertilize. Fork it and rake it down into the soil in preparation for the next crop. With the exception of very long-standing crops, such as parsnips or rutabagas, there always is a chance to grow at least two, often three, occasionally four successive crops on the same ground in a single season. By all means, make the fullest use of your ground. Make it work, but help it along with plenty of manures, composts, and with ample fertilizer and water if needed.

Summer cultivation and summer mulching

Some gardeners grow a clean soil garden, cultivating throughout the season to keep soil loose and weeds down. Others cultivate plants only while in the seedling stage and then go to deep mulch to hold the weeds back; a recent modification of this is the use of plastic sheeting for mulch. In my small garden I hand-hoe or use a small push-plow to keep weeds down throughout the summer except at one end where cucumbers grow on trellises and this area is strawed to a depth of five or six inches when the plants begin to climb. In the big vegetable garden I use the rotary tiller, set very shallow, to run between the rows once each week for good weed control—except in the tomato-growing area, and here, again, I put down a deep straw mulch as soon as the plants begin to flower and go up their stakes. Sometimes I also put straw beneath the squashes and other cucurbits. Summer cultivation should be shallow; if the soil is stirred one inch deep each week you will have no problem at all with weeds. Europeans use special hoes called scuffle hoes which are shoved back and forth just beneath the surface of the soil to cut off all weed seedlings. These are available in this country from garden tool specialists.

I have not been satisfied with the results of plastic mulch. In my area we have hot, dry summers, and the soil temperature beneath the plastic soars. Organic residues in the damp soil go putrid and the odor is unpleasant. Rain falls on a hot day, the sun comes out, and visible steam rises round the leaves of my plants. I have seen fine commercial truck crops grown with plastic mulch in cool climates, but even there I always wonder what is happening to the soil on a long-term basis under such an artificial situation. You may find that plastic mulch is the real answer to weed control and moisture management in your garden. I cannot get along with it.

How to plan a seasonal crop rotation

Every garden soil can stand improving. Vegetable soils, especially, should be exceptionally good, and just right for each kind of vegetable. Some vegetables thrive on manured soils, some do not. Some do best on freshly limed soils, others do not. Some plants need an abundance of fertilizer, others cannot tolerate nutrient-rich soil. The British have worked out excellent rotation systems to account for these various plant needs. The accompanying chart shows a plot over a three-year period with each of three separate sections of the garden receiving a different treatment each year. Yet, over the three years, each section gets "the works."

If you are new to vegetable gardening, you would be wise to start small and add more garden area in years to come. When you build up to three small garden plots (or sections of a single, larger garden), you can use this same rotation system. It is a wonderful way to steadily improve your soil and at the same time give each different kind of vegetable exactly the soil that suits it best. That's good gardening!

First-Year Rotation

Section A
(treat with manures, compost, or peat)

Peas
Beans
Onions
Leeks
Lettuce
Tomatoes
Spinach
Swiss Chard
Celery
Sweet Corn (side-dress)

Succession Crops
Carrots
Beets
Cabbage
Sweet Corn (side-dress)

Section B
(treat with fertilizers and lime)

Cabbage
Brussels Sprouts
Cauliflower
Kale
Broccoli
Kohlrabi
Summer Squash
Winter Squash

Succession Crops
Onions
Sweet Corn
Lima Beans

Section C
(treat with fertilizers)

Potatoes
Carrots
Beets
Parsnips
Rutabagas
Radishes

Succession Crops
Spincah
Lettuce
Chinese Cabbage
Sweet Peppers
Hot Peppers

Second-Year Rotation

Section A
(treat with fertilizers and lime)

Cabbage
Brussels Sprouts
Cauliflower
Kale
Broccoli
Kohlrabi
Summer Squash
Winter Squash

Succession Crops
Onions
Sweet Corn
Lima Beans

Section B
(treat with fertilizers)

Potatoes
Carrots
Beets
Parsnips
Rutabagas
Radishes

Succession Crops
Spinach
Lettuce
Chinese Cabbage
Sweet Peppers
Hot Peppers

Section C
(treat with manures, compost, or peat)

Peas
Beans
Onions
Leeks
Lettuce
Tomatoes
Spinach
Swiss Chard
Celery
Sweet Corn (side dress)

Succession Crops
Carrots
Beets
Cabbage
Sweet Corn (side-dress)

Third-Year Rotation

Section A
(treat with fertilizers)

Potatoes
Carrots
Beets
Parsnips
Rutabagas
Radishes

Succession Crops
Spinach
Lettuce
Chinese Cabbage
Sweet Peppers
Hot Peppers

Section B
(treat with manures, compost, or peat)

Peas
Beans
Onions
Leeks
Lettuce
Tomatoes
Spinach
Swiss Chard
Celery
Sweet Corn (side-dress)

Succession Crops
Carrots
Beets
Cabbage
Sweet Corn (side-dress)

Section C
(treat with fertilizers and lime)

Cabbage
Brussels Sprouts
Cauliflower
Kale
Broccoli
Kohlrabi
Summer Squash
Winter Squash

Succession Crops
Onions
Sweet Corn
Lima Beans

Obviously, this crop-rotation plan does not have to be followed exactly, but it is an excellent guide, and quite reliable so far as it goes. Notice, for example, that cucumbers, salsify, turnips, and endive are not accounted for. How will you know where they fit in? In the A to Z section of this book, soil requirements are given for each vegetable, and that will give you a clue. Also, botanical relationships between vegetables can be used as a guideline: cucumbers are squash relatives and would logically go in the fertilizer-and-lime-treated section each year, as would melons of all sorts. Salsify and turnips are root crops, and as such belong in the fertilizer-treated section with other roots, though turnips also could go with their cabbage relatives in the fertilizer-and-lime section if there is a space problem. Endive, along with escarole, chicory, and other leafy vegetables, belongs in the high humus manures, compost, or peat-treated section. I usually put sweet corn in the fertilizer-and-lime section with outstanding results, because corn, being a grass, thrives on high fertility.

Once you begin working your garden in sections, or maintaining series of small separate garden plots, you will see the difference from year to year as rotation proceeds. It is rather like breaking 80 on the golf course or learning (after ten years of sheer frustration) to lay that dry fly exactly up the riffle from the lunker trout. Vegetable gardening the right way is an even greater accomplishment—there is something on the table every night for your efforts. This year is better than last, and just wait until next year!

A design for a small, long-season garden

A tiny garden plot, one no more than 20 feet long and 15 feet wide, can yield a tremendous volume of produce when pushed to the utmost. This means planting and replanting from early in the spring until fall: cool-weather crops are grown in the spring and fall; hot-weather crops throughout the summer. This size garden is far too small to be cultivated by machine; spading will be sufficient to turn the soil in late fall to fallow over winter, and hand-hoeing to control weeds and maintain loose soil throughout the summer.

This plan originally was developed as a prototype for older persons whose great joy is a bit of daily gardening. It is suitable for any city project, or area where there is limited space available, and for gardeners of all ages—from high school students to those who are retired. Keep in mind that the particular seasonal chart shown is for a Zone 5 (U.S.D.A. Hardiness Zone Map) garden, and must be modified for regional weather and climatic patterns. Farther north, for example, the season would start later and end earlier, and some crops would have to be dropped. In the South, the cool-weather crops would become a year-round winter garden, with a prolonged summer garden.

30

Early Spring Garden
Frost-Free date April 10

Sow seeds and set onions, cabbages and broccoli plants two to four weeks *before* frost-free date (all tolerate some frost) in well-prepared soil. Numbers indicate approximate first to final days for picking. For example, radishes are ready to pull at about 28 days and continue in good condition for about three weeks longer.

$\square$ = 6″

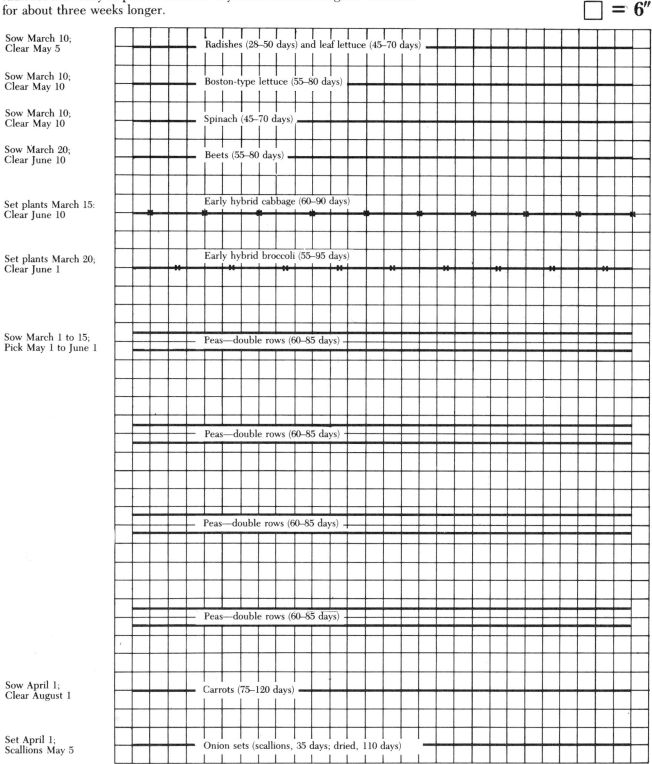

Sow March 10;
Clear May 5
Radishes (28–50 days) and leaf lettuce (45–70 days)

Sow March 10;
Clear May 10
Boston-type lettuce (55–80 days)

Sow March 10;
Clear May 10
Spinach (45–70 days)

Sow March 20;
Clear June 10
Beets (55–80 days)

Set plants March 15:
Clear June 10
Early hybrid cabbage (60–90 days)

Set plants March 20;
Clear June 1
Early hybrid broccoli (55–95 days)

Sow March 1 to 15;
Pick May 1 to June 1
Peas—double rows (60–85 days)

Peas—double rows (60–85 days)

Peas—double rows (60–85 days)

Peas—double rows (60–85 days)

Sow April 1;
Clear August 1
Carrots (75–120 days)

Set April 1;
Scallions May 5
Onion sets (scallions, 35 days; dried, 110 days)

31

Summer Garden

Seeds and plants go in as spring plants are used up. In some cases it is possible to harvest spaced patches of vegetables in a row to allow early setting or seeding of the next crop: for example, cucumbers in leaf lettuce row, tomato plants near cabbages and broccoli plants.

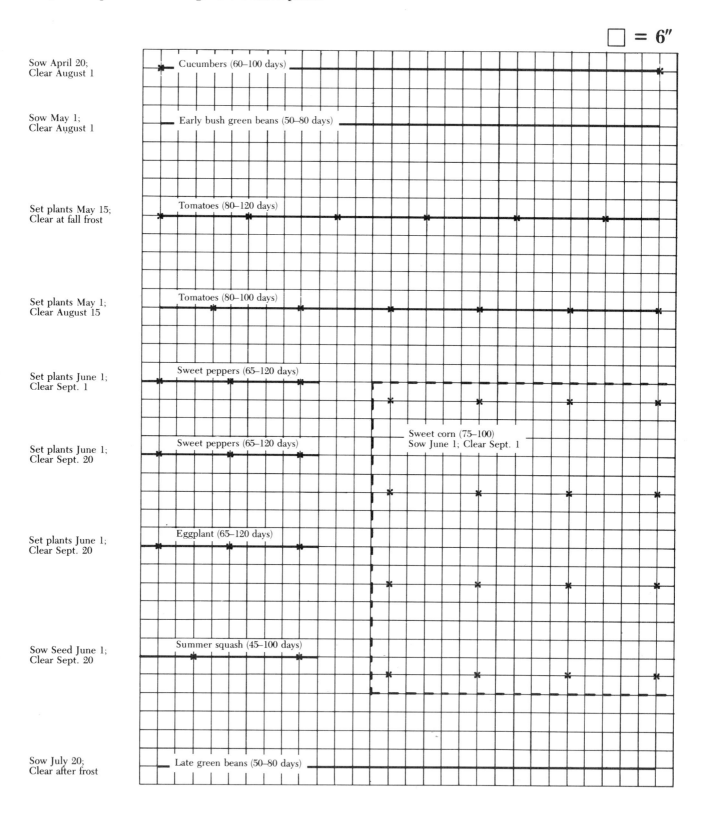

☐ = 6″

Sow April 20;
Clear August 1 — Cucumbers (60–100 days)

Sow May 1;
Clear August 1 — Early bush green beans (50–80 days)

Set plants May 15;
Clear at fall frost — Tomatoes (80–120 days)

Set plants May 1;
Clear August 15 — Tomatoes (80–100 days)

Set plants June 1;
Clear Sept. 1 — Sweet peppers (65–120 days)

Set plants June 1;
Clear Sept. 20 — Sweet peppers (65–120 days)

Sweet corn (75–100)
Sow June 1; Clear Sept. 1

Set plants June 1;
Clear Sept. 20 — Eggplant (65–120 days)

Sow Seed June 1;
Clear Sept. 20 — Summer squash (45–100 days)

Sow July 20;
Clear after frost — Late green beans (50–80 days)

Late Fall — Early Winter Garden

Winter squash, late tomatoes, late beans will be destroyed by the first killing frost. Brussels sprouts, turnips, kohlrabi and spinach will withstand considerable cold weather. Radishes and lettuces will stand frosts but little heavy freezing weather.

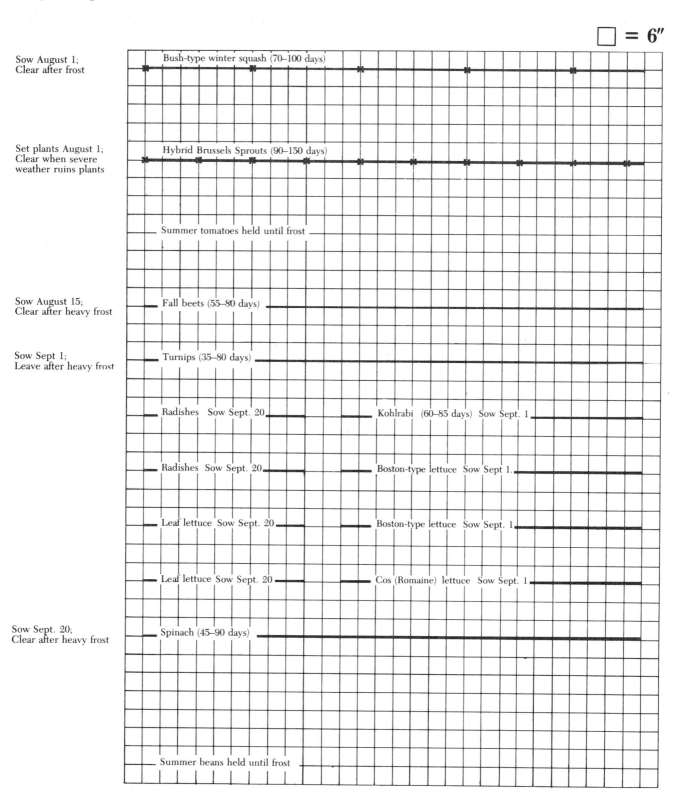

☐ = 6"

Sow August 1;
Clear after frost

Bush-type winter squash (70–100 days)

Set plants August 1;
Clear when severe
weather ruins plants

Hybrid Brussels Sprouts (90–150 days)

Summer tomatoes held until frost

Sow August 15;
Clear after heavy frost

Fall beets (55–80 days)

Sow Sept 1;
Leave after heavy frost

Turnips (35–80 days)

Radishes   Sow Sept. 20

Kohlrabi (60–85 days) Sow Sept. 1

Radishes   Sow Sept. 20

Boston-type lettuce Sow Sept. 1.

Leaf lettuce Sow Sept. 20

Boston-type lettuce   Sow Sept. 1.

Leaf lettuce Sow Sept. 20

Cos (Romaine) lettuce   Sow Sept. 1

Sow Sept. 20;
Clear after heavy frost

Spinach (45–90 days)

Summer beans held until frost

Vegetables from A to Z

Asparagus

Asparagus officinalis   Lily Family

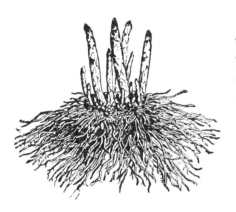

Asparagus probably is the choicest of all permanent vegetables for the home garden. Hardy to sub-zero temperatures, this crop, when well planted and properly cared for, can be expected to produce for 10 to 15 years. Asparagus requires moderately light, very high humus soil that is well drained, moisture-retentive, and fertile. Full sun is essential. Plant a dozen plants for each member of the family, more if you plan to freeze asparagus shoots for out-of-season use.

Soil Preparation

Commercial growers apply at least 30 tons of barnyard manure per acre when preparing soil for asparagus growing. Translated into home-garden measurements, this means at least 40 bushels of manure per 1,000 square feet of asparagus bed. In addition, the application of 40 pounds of 5–10–10 fertilizer per 1,000 square feet insures quick establishment of plants. If your soil is reasonably good loam, spade or trench the soil deeply, turning the above-cited amounts of manure and fertilizer into the top 10 inches. If your soil is heavy or on the clay side, excavate the bed to a depth of 2 feet or more and replace as much as half of it with compost or well-rotted barnyard manure, then add the standard manure and fertilizer applications; incorporate soil, compost, manures, and fertilizer thoroughly. A bed that requires deep preparation should be allowed to settle over winter prior to planting. No asparagus will be harvested during the first two seasons; during these years, apply 5–10–5 fertilizer in early spring, 25 pounds per 1,000 square feet, and in early summer apply an additional dressing of 10 pounds of ammonium nitrate or similar high nitrogen fertilizer. Apply fertilizers as side-dressing, 6 to 8 inches from the plants. Heavier feeding is required for producing beds, as described under "Planting." Asparagus always is maintained in clean cultivation during the winter and spring months; in summer continue clean cultivation or mulch deeply with partially decayed barnyard manure or enriched compost. Never allow the asparagus bed to become weedy, and remove volunteer seedlings as they appear.

Planting

In Europe asparagus usually is grown from seed; in America gardeners usually buy one- or two-year-old plants and set them out. Seed is available from most seed houses and almost every garden shop offers plants in the spring months. To grow your own plants from seed, prepare a rich seedbed in a sunny place. Soak seeds in warm water for two days. Open 2-inch-deep drills 18 inches apart and sow seeds in these rows, spacing them 4 inches apart. Cover to a depth of 1 inch, and as sprouts appear, pull in soil until the drill is filled. Keep plants in clean cultivation; add liquid manure or fertilizer solution at biweekly intervals. Most will bloom before summer is over, and you should discard female plants (those that set berries) as these make slender, stringy shoots when older. Seedlings can be moved to the permanent bed the following spring. A packet of seed yields about 100 plants; an ounce of seed yields about 500 plants. When transplanting seedlings, have the permanent bed ready and the rows opened. Then lift your plants a few at a time, transport them in a basket of barely moist sphagnum moss or compost, and get them into the ground with as little drying as possible.

Purchased plants usually suffer from desiccation. Never pay for plants with shriveled roots. If you must start with plants, buy the one-year-olds; two-year-old plants require just as long to become established, and sometimes they fail, being too large to establish successfully. Plants invariably come from divisions of selected strains, usually from something called "Mary Washington" or "Martha Washington." The correct title is **Mary Washington,** a very good male strain from which selections such as **Viking, Paradise, Washington 500, California U.C.–66,** and **California U.C.–72** have been made. These sometimes are available from seed dealers. Destroy female plants from seedling crops.

With soil deeply prepared, heavily manured and heavily fertilized, planting may proceed. Any number of arrangements may be used in planting; one of the most suitable from a standpoint of cultivation is two rows 18 inches apart, an "alley" of 4 feet, then two more rows. Set plants 18 inches apart in the rows. To plant in average soils, draw open trenches 9 to 10 inches deep; 7 to 8 inches deep in heavier soils. Dress the trench with a layer of sieved compost 1 inch deep, and at each planting station (18-inch intervals, following the above-described system) mound up sieved compost to a depth of 3 or 4 inches. Set a plant centered on each mound, with the roots spread gently over the compost. Cover with 2 or 3 inches of well-crumbled soil. Add soil to the trenches to bring it up to the level of the soil covering the crowns. Trenches still will be several inches below surrounding soil level. As shoots grow, pull in soil until the bed is level.

Cultivation and Management

Keep asparagus beds in clean cultivation, no harvesting through the first two years. Every fall, as the foliage yellows, remove and destroy it (as it harbours rust spores and beetle eggs). Gently cultivate soil over the plants, dress with 2 or 3 inches of partially decayed barnyard manure or enriched compost, and, in colder climates, a further dressing of soil from the alley. These coverings will have to be raked into the alley before growth begins in the spring. Plants always are fertilized in early spring and again as cutting stops. The early application is 15 pounds of 5–10–5 fertilizer per 1,000 square feet; the second is 20 pounds of the same fertilizer plus 5 pounds of superphosphate per 1,000 square feet. The second application encourages strong growth through summer, which enables the plants to store energy foods in the roots for next spring's shoots. Water the asparagus bed during periods of drought.

Begin cutting asparagus in early spring as the first shoots appear. There are two methods. For green shoots, let them grow to a height of 5 to 6 inches, then cut them, slipping the knife into the soil at a forty-five degree angle, about two inches below the ground level. Or, catch them when they are shorter and cut not more than 4 inches below the surface. Some growers who prefer all-white asparagus build up quite a deep mound of partially decayed manure and soil over the rows in the fall and in spring cut through this when a bump indicates that a shoot is about to break through. These mounds are leveled as cutting ceases with the onset of summer—late May to late June, depending on latitude. Cut all shoots during the harvesting season, but stop cutting while shoots are still growing so each plant will mature a number of food-producing stalks over summer.

Pests and Diseases

Asparagus rust is the primary disease of this crop and it is scarcely a problem where resistant strains (such as those mentioned above) are planted. If powdery orange pustules appear on your plants, immediately cut out infected shoots and destroy them. When stalks are always cut in the fall and destroyed, rust seldom becomes a problem. Asparagus beetles are a different thing. There are two sorts, spotted and striped, each about ¼-inch long, rather slender, and quite active. Though the adults and feeding larvae do only moderate damage to vigorous plants, adults lay eggs on burgeoning shoots, and these egg clusters, tightly stuck to shoots just at prime for cutting, make them undesirable. Spray with diazinon or methoxychlor during the summer, but during the cutting season apply only rotenone dust. Destroy all asparagus seedlings in the garden and never allow a beetle population to build up during the summer.

Beans

Broad or Fava Beans

Vicia faba   Legume Family

Broad, or Fava, beans were known to the Egyptians and to the Romans; today they are great favorites in Europe and the Pacific Northwest. Like artichokes and olives, broad beans are an acquired taste, but gardeners in cool, mild climates would be wise to cultivate both the taste and the broad beans themselves because they are easy, prolific, nourishing, and a cool-weather crop that extends through the season. Matter of fact, the best thing about the broad bean is its cold-tolerant growth; in England, gardeners sow a risk crop in November and the main crop in January or February. As seedlings are easily transplanted, you can start them in a chilly cold frame very early and grow them on until danger of heavy frost is over—a necessity if you garden where hot summer weather comes early. If I can spread the broad bean habit to more American gardeners, I shall consider my time well spent. Incidentally, the plants make compost of outstanding quality!

Soil Preparation

A rather heavy, clayish loam is best for broad beans. If your soil is light and sandy, add quantities of strawy manure or coarse compost, and work it deeply for a year or two before trying broad beans. Cabbage-green broad bean plants thrive on soil treated annually to a generous top-dressing of barnyard manure spaded under at least three months before seeding time. If you have to rely on commercial fertilizer, use 5–10–5 and great amounts of organic debris. As with all beans, broad beans "fix" their own nitrogen; phosphate and potash must be supplied by the gardener.

Planting

Sow seed as early in the spring as soil is workable; these will tolerate considerable frost, though not deep freezes. As most strains mature in 65 to 90 days and must have chilly weather throughout the growing season, start seedlings in flats, individual pots, or Jiffy-7's in the cold frame if your warm weather begins too soon after frost is out of the ground. Open 3-inch-deep drills and sow seeds 9 inches apart. If you use a double-row system open drills 9 inches apart, 30 inches between paired rows, and alternate or stagger seeds in the paired rows. Plant seeds treated with the proper nitrogen inoculum for best results. As seedlings appear, begin shallow cultivation and pull soil toward the young plants.

Cultivation and Management

Keep broad beans in clean cultivation, never mulched. The soil should always be somewhat moist; you may have to irrigate during prolonged rainless periods.

Usually broad beans need no fertilizing through the growing period. If the plants seem to lag, open a broad furrow several inches away from the plants (on both sides of the row or rows) and dust in a mixture of three parts superphosphate and one part potash (muriate of potassium), 2 ounces per yard. Cover the fertilizer with soil.

Most people tend to pick broad beans when they are overripe. You may gather very tender young pods to cook whole, or better, wait until the beans are almost full-sized and succulent, shell them like fresh lima beans, and prepare according to north European or Italian recipes. Delicious!

Pests and Diseases

Pea aphids seem to find broad beans as soon as they emerge from the ground, even during quite cold weather. Spray with malathion or diazinon, adding a sticker-spreader to the solution, or dust with an all-purpose vegetable garden dust while dew is on the plants. If the aphid population seems particularly persistent, after a good crop of pods has set, pinch out the top of each plant to discourage the pests.

Cultivars

Unless you buy from a European seed house, probably you will have to settle for **Broad Windsor Long Pod,** maturing in 65 days, with large beans in long pods on sturdy, upright-growing plants. Favored short-podded, small-seeded English varieties include **Early Magazan, Fan,** and **Green Gem.** Long-podded favorites include **Seville Long Pod, Aqua Dulce,** and the various selections of **Exhibition Long Pod.** In England there are many strains of the Windsor type.

Bush (Snap) and Pole Beans

Phaseolus vulgaris   Legume Family

Pole beans and bush beans produce succulent, rather fleshy pods which vegetable growers harvest while young and tender for table use. Relatives of these familiar beans are the kidney beans, pinto beans, black beans, navy beans, and other sorts grown for harvest when dry. Generally speaking, the home-owner does best to raise only the green-picked sorts as growing beans, for drying requires field conditions and a rather dry, bright climate. Beans are an easy to grow, nutritious crop. Properly grown, they are subject to few ills and pests. While canned green beans once were a household staple from the garden, today freezing is much easier and quicker, and yields a higher quality product. A few bush beans belong in every garden, even where there is no vegetable garden, as the plants can be tucked in among the annuals in a sunny border.

Soil Preparation

Beans thrive in average garden loam prepared as outlined in the section on Soil Preparation and Management, page 17. Bean seeds germinate quickly and cultivation should begin immediately as plants thrive in soil that is kept loose at the surface. Never work your bean plants (cultivation or harvest) while plants are moist from dew, rain, or overhead irrigation, as this brings on disease. Restrict bean hoeing and picking to afternoon and early evening hours. Weekly cultivation keeps down weeds and maintains loose soil conducive to strong bean plant roots. If you are a mulcher, maintain a band of cultivated soil on both sides of the bean rows and mulch the space between the rows. Bean plants deeply embedded in straw or other mulch almost always develop leaf fungus lesions and spotted pods.

Planting

After danger of frost is past, open bean rows on 24- to 30-inch centers. A good method is to open a 6-inch-wide row about 4 inches deep. Dress the bottom of the row with 5–10–5 fertilizer, 3 to 5 ounces per yard depending on soil fertility, and cover the fertilizer with 3 inches of soil. With the back of the rake lightly tamp the soil, and down the middle of the inch-deep trench plant a row of beans, spacing them 3 to 4 inches apart. Cover the seeds not more than 1 inch deep, shallower in heavy soil. As leaf fungi and root decaying organisms are major problems with beans, it is best always to plant treated seed; the usual treatment is a fungicide such as Captan. *Treated seed will be colored, usually bright pink, and is unfit for human, bird, or animal consumption.* Beans are a hot-weather crop. You can begin sowing when your soil thermometer indicates 60° F. at 3 inches, but seeds will sprout faster at a soil temperature of 65° F. Make repeated plantings every ten days to two weeks to within about eight weeks of the first frost date in your area. Often very late planted beans come along very quickly as soil is hot and fall rains encourage fast growth. Though our first average frost date is about October 20, I have picked beans the first week in November that were of better quality than the summer ones. In any case, if frost catches the crop, the soil is better for having supported the nitrogen-fixing plants for a few weeks, and the plants make marvelous compost.

Cultivation and Management

Thin bush beans to stand 9 to 12 inches apart in the row before they begin to crowd. As production begins, pick beans frequently to encourage blossom set and prolonged production. If your soil is quite poor, as plants begin to bloom, apply a band of 5–10–5 fertilizer 6 inches wide 4 inches away from the plants on both sides of the row. Scratch this in. Use about 2 ounces per yard of band. Fertilizer must never be allowed to touch the plants *or bean plant roots* as they are extremely sensitive. As production slows, pick the remaining crop and pull up the plants for composting. It is best to rely on successive plantings rather than to try keeping a single planting in prolonged production. Where the beans grew, fork up the soil and plant a succession crop. In mid-summer, plant late bush squash, fall potatoes, or set plants of late tomatoes or peppers. Later in the season follow up a bean crop with fall lettuces, spinach, Chinese cabbage or regular fall cabbage, carrots, beets, or a similar crop tolerant of cold weather.

Pests and Diseases

Bean crops often fail because seed is planted in soggy soil or in soil that is too cold. Under these conditions seed decays before or after it sprouts. Captan, a common seed treatment chemical mentioned previously, inhibits some of the decay, but is not entirely foolproof if conditions are too bad. Do not worry about Captan interfering with soil bacteria. It does not appreciably disturb beneficial soil microflora (bacteria and fungi), and will not harm a bird that finds an occasional treated seed. Once plants are above ground various leaf spots and anthracnose may be a problem, particularly if plants are disturbed while the foliage is damp. Avoid overly lush foliage due to heavy applications of high-nitrogen fertilizers. All-purpose garden dust will offer some protection during rainy, humid periods.

Mexican bean beetles are the worst scourge. They are round insects, about ¼ inch across, of a dirty yellow-orange color with black markings. The larvae are orangish, humped creatures with tufts of hairs. These chew away bean foliage, flowers, and fruits. Before bloom period use methoxychlor; after beans begin to set use malathion, diazinon, or, safest of all, rotenone. In late summer or early fall grasshoppers may be a problem. The above-listed insecticides give some control; non-bearing young plants may be sprayed with a stomach poison such as arsenate of lead or use toxaphene, but never use these when beans are beginning to form. When a bean planting dwindles, immediately pull plants for fast composting so pests and diseases will not incubate on old plants.

Cultivars

Astro, 49 days; 5½–6¼-inch oval pods.
Bush Blue Lake 274, 58 days; 5½–6½-inch round pods.
Contender, 40 days; 5½-inch oval pods.
Executive, 46 days; 6-inch round pods.
Greensleeves, 56 days; 5½–6-inch round pods.
Improved Tendergreen, 45 days; 6–7-inch round pods.

Lima Beans, Bush and Pole

Phaseolus limensis   Legume Family

Lima beans, both bush and pole, belong only in a large garden because they require a long season to produce, are space-consuming, and plants yield modestly. But freshly picked limas are among the best-tasting vegetables, so grow them if you have the space available. Coming from tropical regions, limas can be planted successfully only after the soil is thoroughly warmed. They require a deeply dug, moderately fertile, fast-draining loam, and full sun. You will need about ten bush plants or ten pole plants for each adult member of the family, more if you plan to freeze beans for winter consumption.

Soil Preparation

Any well-drained garden soil, from sandy loam to clay loam, suits lima beans, but drainage is critical—limas will not tolerate soggy soil. All bean roots may be damaged by contact with fertilizers, so plant where a highly fertilized crop such as tomatoes, potatoes, or sweet corn grew the previous year, or top-dress the soil early in the season before forking so that by planting time the fertilizer will be distributed through the soil.

Planting

When soil temperature has reached at least 65° F., plant the lima beans. Open drills for bush limas with 30-inch centers, and sow seeds at about 5-inch intervals; cover with 1½ inches of pulverized soil and gently compact by tamping with the back of a steel rake. If soil is dry at planting time, flood the open drill with water and allow it to soak away; sow seeds on damp soil and cover with dry soil, then tamp. As seedlings develop their second set of true leaves, thin seedlings to stand 10 to 12 inches apart. All lima beans need lots of room for good results. To grow pole-type limas, set 8-foot poles 3 feet apart in a row, or set two parallel rows and pull four poles together to make a "teepee." Rough-sawn wood or saplings with rough bark are best for pole beans as they are weak climbers. At the base of each pole plant, plant four or five beans; thin to not more than three as they develop.

By all means, treat your seed with an appropriate nitrogen inoculum for optimum root development. Most lima beans germinate in five or six days and reach the four-leaf stage (for thinning) in about two weeks. Avoid over-fertilization; where soil is lean, open a hoe-wide, shallow trench on each side of the bean row, 2 inches from the plant stems, and dust in 3 ounces of 5–10–5 fertilizer divided between the trenches on both sides of the bean row. Cover the fertilizer. A single fertilizing as bean plants begin to branch usually suffices.

Cultivation and Management

Lima beans come along slowly. Baby limas mature in about 60 days, Fordhooks are ready to pick in about 72 days, and most pole limas require about 85 days to reach maturity. Limas are easily grown in clean cultivation; with a conventional garden hoe or a Dutch (scuffle) hoe stir the soil shallowly at least once each week. Avoid deep cultivation which will injure spreading roots. Where summers are hot and dry a porous summer mulch may be applied, but only after the soil temperature reaches 75°F. Loose straw or weed-free hay is ideal for this purpose. Coarse compost also is suitable. Water by ground irrigation, but not more than once or twice each week. Limas grow best on the dry side. During very hot weather blossoms will fall rather than making pods, but with the onset of cooler weather a generous crop of pods will appear.

Most gardeners prefer to pick lima beans when the seeds are full and meaty but still succulent. Wait until you can feel a quite plump bean inside the leathery pod before harvesting. Lima beans can also be left on the plant until the pods dry; these are then shelled out to be further air-dried, then stored as dry beans.

Pests and Diseases

Lima beans may suffer from various fungus ills, especially when germinating and at the seedling stage. Best results come when fungicide-treated (usually pink-colored) seeds are planted; *a fungicide often used, called "Captan," renders the beans unfit for human, animal, or bird consumption.* (However, Captan is not considered toxic to wildlife or injurious to soil ecology). From mid-summer onward watch for bean beetles and other gnawing pests; eliminate these with diazinon or with a rotenone or pyrethrum spray or dust. As with other bean plants, do not disturb the foliage of lima beans when it is dew-covered.

In general, lima bean plants grown on rather lean soil in full sun are a healthy dark green, virtually impervious to diseases.

Soy or Soja Beans

Glycine max   Legume Family

Grown as a food plant in China and Japan for thousands of years, the soybean is known to Americans as a farm crop used largely for animal feed. In recent years protein-rich soybeans have been the source of raw materials for the plastics industry. Today, Americans are learning to eat soybeans. These abundant-producing legumes are easy to grow and free of most pests and diseases, but they may have an unusual flavor to some and take considerable getting used to.

Soil Preparation

Any general garden soil in full sun will produce a crop of soybeans. The plants do best in deeply dug, very well-drained soil that is moderately fertile, with ample phosphorus and potash. If possible, grow soybeans where corn was grown, chopped up and spaded under the previous year. In spring, dress the soil prior to spading with 3 ounces per square yard of a mixture of three parts superphosphate and one part potash (muriate of potassium). Do not plant until the soil is warmed to at least 65° F.

Planting

Mark off rows on 24-inch centers and open drills 3 inches deep. Inoculate seeds with soybean nitrogen inoculum and sow seeds 4 inches apart. When the hairy little plants begin to branch, thin to 10 to 12 inches. At this time, pull soil from midway between rows toward the plants, hilling to a depth of 2 inches. Soybeans seldom need additional water, but during a prolonged drought soak the soil between the rows deeply.

Cultivation and Management

With a hoe or pronged cultivator, keep the soil between soybean rows loose to a depth of 2 inches. Avoid using any sort of mulch as this holds moisture which invites various leaf fungi and serves as a breeding place for insect pests.

Soybeans are a long season proposition, taking from twelve to fifteen weeks to make a mature crop. There are two ways of using soybeans: when beans in the pod are fully developed but still green, they may be shelled out to be cooked as you would limas; or allow the pods to dry on the plant, and then shell out the dry beans for use in various ways. Green or dried soybean plants are a wonderful addition to the compost heap.

Pests and Diseases

Normally no pests or diseases harass vigorous-growing soybean plants. But if pests or disease appears, dust or spray with an all-purpose vegetable garden fungicide-insecticide mixture. The most common and not too serious pest is the aphid, easily controlled with malathion or diazinon.

Cultivars

At least two sorts are available on the American market: *Early Green Bush,* 85 days; 4-inch-long green pods, 3 beans per pod.
Kanrich, 103 days; pods as above, but plants larger and coarser.

Beets

Beta vulgaris   Goosefoot Family

The beet is one of the oldest cultivated vegetables, and today appears in several forms. Bunching beets are grown primarily for their foliage (beet greens); canning beets are important for the fleshy root which almost always is eaten cooked; in agriculture the mangel-wurzel (cow beet) is a source of winter fodder; and the sugar beet yields table sugar and other products. The chards, too, are a form of *B. vulgaris*. Beets are reasonably cold-hardy, rather intolerant of hot, dry weather, and grow in a fairly wide range of garden soils. Beet "seeds" actually are clusters of seeds, tightly adherent unless you buy the very expensive Mono-germ strains which normally are grown only by truck gardeners who can no longer afford the high cost of hand-thinning. The quality of beet roots suffers if the temperature drops below 50°F. for any length of time, and during hot, dry weather beet roots have a low sugar content and the roots may be zoned red and white rather than deep red throughout.

Soil Preparation

As for all root crops, soil for beets should be deeply dug, well-drained, and uniform. Streaks of fertilizers or soil additives produce malformed, often off-flavor roots. Not tolerant of alkaline soil, beets grow best in circumneutral to slightly acid soils; the recommended pH is 6.0 to 6.8. While beets will grow in stony soil, often they are somewhat dimpled due to crowding against stones while increasing in girth. Beets grow well in sandy loam, silt, or muck soils, but often make malformed roots in heavy clay soil. Dress beet soil with 2 or 3 inches of well-rotted barnyard manure and turn it under at least a month before planting time; or put down 5–10–5 fertilizer at about 5 ounces per square yard (30 to 40 pounds per 1,000 square feet).

Planting

Begin to sow seed in early spring, at least two weeks before the frost-free date; and continue with successive plantings at two-week intervals. An ounce of beet seed sows a 100-foot row. Beet seedlings appear in clusters (except from the Mono-germ strains); spacing is important. Sow seeds sparsely in rows spaced 12 to 14 inches apart and cover with ½ to ¾-inch of soil, the shallower planting in heavier soils. Germination usually begins in four or five days and is complete in ten days to two weeks. Thin 8-inch-tall plants and use for table greens (or discard them) so beets develop 3 to 4 inches apart. It is not necessary to thin seedlings of beets grown only for greens.

Cultivation and Management

Maintain a loose soil "mulch" in the beet bed. Beets grown for bunching (greens) reach maturity in about seven weeks, others in six to nine weeks, depending on the variety. For best quality, plants must grow quickly and steadily; maintain nearly constant soil moisture by overhead watering if necessary. When plants are about 7 inches high, side-dress with nitrate of soda at the rate of 7 or 8 ounces per 100 feet of row, dividing the application between both sides of the row. Scratch in this fertilizer about 2 inches from the plants. If insect pests gnaw foliage, apply a control chemical (see below) quickly as healthy, vigorous foliage is essential for the production of tender, fiber-free roots. Begin harvesting beets when walnut-sized by pulling every other plant; use these small beets for pickling, the remaining beets quickly will grow to slicing size.

Pests and Diseases

Few pests and diseases attack beets, but beet leaf miner and beet webworm may be a problem, and in late summer blister beetles can quickly defoliate an entire planting. If beet foliage is gnawed from beneath or if miner larvae make zigzag tunnels between the two layers of the leaf, spray with diazinon, rotenone, pyrethrum, or other vegetable garden insecticide. In damp springs, beet leaf spot may mar the foliage; dead patches of tissue surrounded by a purple zone are symptoms of the disease. As soon as the first spots appear, spray beet foliage with manzate, ferbam, or zineb according to the manufacturer's instructions. But beets often are relatively free from attack by pests and diseases. In full sun, in fertile, well-drained soil, beets usually come to maturity with no difficulties.

Cultivars

Dozens of cultivated varieties of beets are in the seed catalogs. Among the best are:

Early Sorts
Crosby Egyptian, 42 days.
Early Red Ball, 38 days.
Egypt Select, 38 days.
Little Egypt, 34 days.
Stokes Special Early, 35 days.

Main Crop
Detroit Dark Red, 45 days.
Garnet, 45 days.
King Red, 45 days.
Redpak, 43 days.
Ruby Queen, 41 days.
Spring Red, 48 days.
Vermilion, 46 days.

For Greens (but with a good quality, small root)
Green Top Bunching, 48 days.

Several Novelty Beets, some quite tasty, have been introduced in recent years:
Burpee's Golden Beet, 50 days; bright gold-colored root. Good.
Formanova, 46 days; a cylindrical beet of good quality; hill this one or the top of the root will sunscald.
Long Season or **Winter Keeper,** 78 days. This is a large, rough, ugly beet with the finest flavor, in my estimation, of all beets. It stands through heat, is good from early to late in the season, and is my main crop!

Broccoli

*Brassica oleracea (**Cymosa**)* and   Mustard Family
B. oleracea var. *italica (**Calabrese**)*

In Europe north of the Alps broccoli of the single-headed sort is sometimes included with cauliflowers. In America the heading sorts are considered as broccoli and the branching sorts, equally common, are referred to as "sprouting broccoli" or as "Calabrese," and that occasionally leads to "Italian sprouting broccoli." Whatever you call it, you should grow it. The broccolis are easy and the yield is plentiful. For the home garden I certainly recommend the sprouting (side-shoot) types or, better, the newest hybrids which tend to make a large, central head followed by a fine crop of side-shoots which break a few days after the central head is cut.

Soil Preparation

Soil requirements are the same as for cabbage; nearly any soil will do, if worked up correctly. Texture is less important than ample fertility and a constant supply of moisture during the growing season. As cabbage, broccoli does best on tight soil.

Planting

Schedule two crops each year to take advantage of cool, damp weather in spring and fall. Sow spring seed eight to ten weeks before your frost-free date in a flat or a cold frame. Transplant seedlings at the two-leaf stage to a frame bed or to pots. Protect seedlings from heavy frost but grow them cold. Usually when well hardened they can go to the open garden two to four weeks before the frost-free date as they are tolerant of light frost. Treat the fall crop similarly; sow seed after mid-summer, grow seedlings as cool as possible (under lights in the basement), and protect them from insect pests. Set well-started plants into the garden in rows 3 feet apart; plants 18 inches apart in each row, staggered in adjacent rows if convenient. With the fall crop, work up the soil, water it well unless it is amply moist, and when it is again workable, set in young plants. Mulch between rows to keep soil as cool as possible, and water lightly but frequently until the weather cools.

Cultivation and Management

As for cabbage, broccoli does best if cultivated regularly, shallowly, and with an occasional application of fertilizer through the growing season. (*See* Cabbage for further details.)

Broccoli is ready to cut when the central head is 6 to 9 inches across (smaller sizes for some hybrids and "sprouting" kinds; larger for the "heading" sorts). Cut the head with a sharp knife; broadcast a handful of 5–8–7 fertilizer (if you can't find it, use 10–10–10) around the base of the plant, scratch it in, and water thoroughly. In a few days side-sprouts will begin to break.

Pests and Diseases

Pests and diseases of broccoli are the same as those for cabbage. Especially troublesome are the various "worms", which are actually larvae of cabbage loopers and similar moths, and may work deep into the heads. Frequent applications of pyrethrum or rotenone control these; use Dylox on small plants if many white butterflies are in the garden. Malathion reduces aphid infestations.

Cultivars

Among the open-pollinated sorts are:

De Cicco, 60 days; very early, rather loose-headed sort which produces side-shoots later; its chief merit is earliness.

Green Mountain, 85 days; tight blue-green heads with medium-sized laterals; stands well in heat.

Italian Sprouting (Calabrese), 80 days; produces a large, rather loose central head followed by a strong crop of medium-sized laterals.

Rapine (Spring Raab), 70 days; an early branching sort that never forms a central head; bolts early in heat; must be kept moist.

Spartan Early, 76 days; smallish plants with quite large central heads; a good choice for home gardens.

The recently introduced hybrid broccolis are best for the home gardener; they bear very heavily on moderate-sized plants and are uniform. Because the seed comes from an elaborate closed-pollination breeding program it is expensive, but worth every penny.

Bravo, 76 days; a smallish plant with a 9-inch, dense central head; ideal for cooler climates.

Cleopatra, 75 days; outstanding for flavor, earliness and

quality; very productive with a large central head and vigorous side-shoots.

Green Comet, 78 days; a moderate-sized head of superior quality, followed by very good laterals; plants are almost blue. My favorite strain for Midwest growing.

Premium Crop, 82 days; an award-winning strain with huge, top-quality central heads; no laterals ever form; harvest the crop and remove plants for a follow-up vegetable. A good home garden sort.

Brussels Sprouts

Brassica oleracea var. *gemmifera*   Cabbage Family

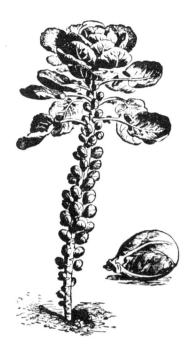

This member of the cabbage family has been traced back to fourteenth-century cultivation near Brussels, Belgium. Today it is a major fall and winter vegetable in all of Europe and is gaining in popularity in the United States, primarily due to its availability as a first-rate frozen product. There is a trick to growing a fine crop of rock-hard sprouts. Plant them in rich, deeply worked, rather tight soil with ample spacing between plants, and ram them in! That is, as the plants begin to grow, trod down the soil tightly around each one. Hand-pull weeds; avoid cultivating deeper than half an inch. If the soil is hard and tight, the sprouts will be firm and delicious, but if the soil is light and loose (or fluffy from too recent manuring), the sprouts will be "blowers"— hollow masses of loose leaves with no delicious core of blanched tissue.

Soil Preparation

Determine your brussels sprouts' planting area in the fall; rather than a single long row, plant in a rectangular area for better management. Avoid adding manures or compost to the soil, but dress it with a ureaform nitrogen formulation of 5–8–7 fertilizer, 5 ounces per square yard. Deeply spade or double-dig the area (fertilize only the top spit). In this case, fork over the topsoil in the fall so winter will settle it in tightly. In spring, rake down the soil and sow a quick "catch crop" of early peas or lettuce; this has to be harvested and out of the way for the brussels sprouts plants to be set in during June.

Planting

About mid-May, sow brussels sprout seeds in an outdoor seedbed; any freshly turned, friable soil will do. Open drills ½ inch deep on 4- to 6-inch centers and sow seeds three or four per inch. Thin to an inch apart at the four-leaf stage. Watch for cutworms. When seedlings are four to five weeks old, lift with as much soil as possible and transplant to the garden. Mark off rows on 36-inch centers and set plants 24 inches apart in each row, staggering them if convenient. Water in the transplants with a transplant-type fertilizer such as Transplantone and begin a weekly spray program using a malathion-methoxychlor mixture to control aphids and cabbage loopers. When seedlings appear to be established, tread down the soil around each one so it is firm.

Cultivation and Management

Shallow cultivation for weed control is permissible, at least in early summer; avoid cultivation to any depth. It is best to hand-weed plants so soil remains compact. If additional watering is required, runoff will be a problem on the tight soil; a very slow sprinkling is preferable. By mid-summer a porous mulch (loose straw) may be applied to a depth of 6 inches; keep it a few inches from the plants.

Toward mid-summer small sprouts will begin to appear near the base of the plants. As these appear, with a sharp knife cut away the lowest leaves, two or three at a time, leaving the sprouts unharmed. Gradually remove the leaves, working up the stem until just a crown is left at the top by mid-September. At this time, nip out the growing tip (preserving the umbrella of upper leaves) which encourages rapid development of the sprouts all down the stem. Harvest sprouts from the bottom up.

Pick sprouts when they are solid, about 1 inch in diameter; the older varieties may be gathered in four to five pickings, but the newest hybrid sorts from Europe may be picked at once or in two harvests—a bonus if you wish to freeze them for later use. All brussels sprouts are sweeter if harvested after a light frost or two. Where winter comes late, after a few frosts mound the plants loosely with straw so the winter sun cannot burn them and leave the crop in the garden until a deep freeze is imminent.

Cultivars

Among the older open-pollinated sorts are:
Early Morn, 105 days; plants are compact, pyramid-shaped; sprouts large, elliptical.
Green Pearl, 120 days; a very popular sort; upright, sprouts globe-shaped, medium-green, very solid.
Long Island Improved, 115 days; several choice strains have been selected out, plants are too wide for home growing; sprouts globe-shaped, medium-green.
The newer, hybrid brussels sprouts, usually F_1 hybrids and therefore expensive, are particularly valuable for the home garden for their smaller-sized plants and heavy production of exceptionally high-quality sprouts.
Indra, 128 days; a European hybrid producing globe-

shaped, medium-green, very solid sprouts, usually in early October.

Jade Cross, 95 days; a short plant producing nearly twice as many sprouts as the open-pollinated sorts. Sprouts are medium-sized, dark green, oval. The most popular for American gardens today.

Jade Cross E, 97 days; much like the above, but plants slightly taller, suitable for heavier cropping.

Peer Gynt, 135 days; a very high-yielding European sort, producing round, dark-green sprouts; favored for freezing.

Topscore, 138 days; the latest brussels sprout cultivar from Europe, produces round, dark-green sprouts; rock-hard.

Cabbage

Brassica oleracea var. *capitata*   Mustard Family

A northern species, thriving in a cool, moist climate, cabbage is a winter crop in the south and is planted for spring, summer, and early fall in the north. Where summers are hot, cabbages can be grown in spring and fall. Where climates are relatively mild the year round (as in the Pacific Northwest) cabbage is a year-round crop in the open garden. Today hundreds of varieties of cabbages are available to the gardener—a bewildering array. Some of the more hardy types are intended for the commercial market. Others are for pickling (sauerkraut manufacture), still others are for home use in coleslaw, salads, and cooked dishes. Because cabbage was known as a first-rate winter vegetable for centuries, early commerical plant breeders converted it from a choice table vegetable to a virtually indestructible storage and shipping sales piece. Many modern strains exhibit vestiges of this remarkable durability. The choicest table cabbages are the delicate new F_1 hybrid strains—leafy, tender, and sweet-flavored, and the Savoy cabbages. These must go directly from garden to table, they wilt and deteriorate in a few hours. If you are not yet a cabbage fancier, grow a crop of **Emerald Cross Hybrid** or **Savoy King.** You will be delighted with the succulence and delicacy of these fragile cultivars.

Soil Preparation

Cabbage will grow on almost any soil provided that it is naturally on the alkaline side or has been limed in the last year or two. Commercially, early cabbages are produced on the lighter, sandy-loam soils while late cabbage is planted on heavier soils which maintain moisture better. One expert claims that consistent moisture and relatively high soil fertility are more important to a good cabbage crop than soil texture. The minerals cabbages need most are nitrogen and potash. For optimum production, in the fall deeply turn the soil, incorporating as much compost or barnyard manure as is available. In the spring fork under 30 to 40 pounds of 10–10–10 fertilizer per 1,000 square feet. Even this heavy fertilizer application will need to be supplemented with additional nutrients as the crop grows.

Planting

List your seasonal cabbage needs to give you an idea of how to schedule your crops. For just table consumption, one to two dozen plants maturing in the spring and early summer, followed by a similar number maturing in the fall, are plenty. If some sauerkraut is to be prepared, you may need an additional twenty heads or so; these ought to be the larger, firmer, sort.

My preference is as follows: at least a dozen heads of a succulent, early hybrid sort for table use and for freezing. A dozen or so Savoys for special table use (cabbage rolls, stuffed cabbage), and to give to friends who are not familiar with this delicious cabbage. A few red cabbages, *not* the storage sort—because they are so handsome in the garden and because they are essential for that fine German dish, sweet-sour cabbage. Several large, solid-headed cabbages, coming on late, for sauerkraut. Finally, if space allows, a few of those strange winter-storage cabbages, just to see how long they really will keep in the cellar. So far, October heads have held a reasonably good quality through April! That adds up to a lot of cabbage; far too much to plant at one time. I divide up the crop, some for spring, some for late summer. Even so, we give away quite a lot of cabbage.

It becomes expensive to buy packets of seeds of so many different kinds of cabbages; also, a packet produces over 100 plants. A good solution is to work out an arrangement with two or three neighbors and buy seeds on shares. Decide on mutually satisfactory cultivars and either divide up the seeds (I find this best) or let each person start plants of one or two kinds at appropriate times for everybody.

The nitty-gritty of growing cabbages from seed is simple. In a flat or bulb pan filled with seed compost or a synthetic seed germinating medium, sow seeds ½ inch apart. Cover with ¼ inch of soil or germinating medium, and hold at warm room temperature. Seeds germinate in four to five days; grow the seedlings in very bright light in a cool place. Transplant to individual pots at the two-leaf stage; never allow young cabbage plants to become pot-bound.

If you can, start seedlings indoors and transplant them to a frost-free cold frame. Sow seeds six to eight weeks before the frost-free date for the early spring crop; and from mid-July to mid-August for the fall crop, depending on when your garden soil begins to cool. Our summers are hot so I start all my fall cabbages—broccoli, cauliflower, and the like—in the cool basement under fluorescent lights.

Set out cabbage plants beginning two or three weeks

before the frost-free date (earlier if you can cover young plants on frosty nights and uncover them each morning). Space cabbage rows 24 to 36 inches apart; small-headed hybrids usually are planted on 18-inch centers, the larger Ballhead and Savoy kinds go on 24- to 36-inch centers.

Cultivation and Management

Cabbages are a high-maintenance crop. Trod in the seedlings as cabbages do best in tight soil. Grow in clean cultivation, but merely scratch the surface with a scuffle hoe or a rake to keep weed seedlings down. Do not mulch cabbages; this encourages slugs and snails which eat into the heads from below. Use poison bait for these pests.

As the crop comes on, side-dress plants at four-week intervals with ½ ounce of nitrate of soda per yard of row (or in a wide band around each plant at least 8 inches from the stalk). Scratch in this fertilizer.

Where spring is short and hot weather comes early, take care to keep cabbage soil uniformly moist. If soil dries out and then water is applied (irrigation or rainfall) the cabbage heads resume growth quickly and almost always split, and split heads have to be harvested immediately as they decay fast.

Cabbages can be harvested any time after the heads are fully formed. Tender young cabbages are a great table delicacy. For sauerkraut or for winter storage leave the heads on the plants as long as possible to achieve maximum size and maturity.

Pests and Diseases

Cabbage "worms" and cabbage loopers are the chief pests of the cabbage patch. A rotenone or pyrethrum spray or dust will protect the plants; add a sticker-spreader to any spray as cabbage leaves are waxy. I have found that a weekly spray of Dylox (follow the manufacturer's instructions exactly) controls most above-ground pests on cabbage plants; but spraying must stop not less than three weeks prior to harvest. Then shift to the less effective, but nontoxic rotenone or pyrethrum. Dylox also cuts down on the hard-to-kill harlequin plant bugs (related to stink bugs), which are so damaging late in the season.

Other cabbage ailments include bacterial black spot and blackleg, a virus disease called "cabbage yellows" and club root. Root maggots and cabbage aphids also may be a problem. But these are not common; if you encounter them, call your County Horticulturist at the Extension Agent's office for specific controls developed for local conditions.

Cultivars

A good way to decide on spring and fall cabbages for your area is to talk with local gardeners; there are so many cultivars on the market that a list is almost meaningless. Here are a few sorts especially suitable for home growing:

Early Strains, Open-Pollinated
Early Greenball, 63 days; a small English strain; heads to 2½ pounds; not yellows-tolerant.
Early Marvel, 65 days; dark green, heads to 4 pounds, not disease resistant.
Emerald Acre, 61 days; best flavor of open-pollinated sorts, not yellows-resistant.
Golden Acre, 65 days; modern-sized, looser than some, high yellows resistance.
Jersey Wakefield, 65 days; conical heads, noted quality; some strains show yellows resistance.

Early Hybrid Strain (Best for Home Use)
Emerald Cross, 63 days; 3 pounds; brilliant green interior, blue-green wrapper leaves; not yellows-tolerant.

Second Early Hybrid Strains
Canada Kraut, 66 days; solid, globe-shaped heads, yellows-tolerant.
Princess, 66 days; similar to the above, too loose for kraut but superb for table use.
Stonehead, 67 days; old standby strain, yellows-tolerant.

Mid-season Cabbage, Open-Pollinated
Copenhagen Market, 70 days; with early and late strains, round-headed, fine-flavored; not yellows-tolerant.
Early Round Dutch, 71 days; firm, round heads, good for close planting; not yellows-resistant.
Wisconsin Ballhead, 90 days; 8-pound heads, choice for sauerkraut, yellows-tolerant; does not store.

Late Cabbage, Open-Pollinated

Baby Head, 70 days; 2¼ pounds, round and solid, not yellows–tolerant.

Penn State Ballhead, 90 days; a medium-sized, very firm cabbage, good for sauerkraut; not yellows-tolerant.

Green Cabbage for Late Storage

Introduced to America in the late 1960's, these strains of cabbage behave oddly. Unlike most cabbages which "bleed" readily when cut, the juice of these coagulates. From experience I can recommend only:

Ultra Green, 99 days; bright green, good flavor; sow for maturing after a light frost or two; store cool.

Red Cabbage

The traditional commercial red cabbage is **Mammoth Red Rock,** a fine vegetable; but for the home garden try:

Meteor, 80 days; brightly colored, superior flavor, easy to grow.

Red Head, 85 days; a closed-pollinated sort, fine quality, yellows-tolerant.

Savoy Cabbage

These are far more delicate in flavor and texture than any other cabbage. Intolerant of storage, they seldom reach the market. The traditional one is **Chieftain Savoy.** For the home garden plant:

Savoy King, 86 days; a closed-pollinated hybrid yielding flat globe heads, dark green outside, white within. Not yellows-tolerant. If you plant only one kind of cabbage, this is it!

Cantaloupe *(See* MELONS: Muskmelon, page 106.)

Carrot

Daucus carota var. *sativa*   Carrot Family

In mild climates where the soil does not freeze in winter and summer is not too hot, fresh carrots may be grown in the garden the year round. The rest of us have to grow our carrots when the climate is right—cool and mild. Usually, this means a spring crop and a fall crop. But, by choosing strains that do not go pithy or dull-tasting in heat, I also have added carrots to my mid-summer garden.

Carrots come in various forms and colors. Today, most are orange. In very old catalogs some were described as yellow, others as red. But today carrot forms vary widely, from the long, narrow, tapering roots to small ball-shaped cultivars. The trick with carrots is to find the ones adaptable to your soil and weather. Not every soil is conducive to producing those long, slender, Imperial Valley supermarket carrots; but you might come up with a carrot that is far more flavorful.

Soil Preparation

Light, sandy loam produces the best carrots. If your soil is a heavier sort, make up the difference with extremely deep cultivation. Where carrots are grown commercially—on light, sandy loam—special plows break the soil to a depth of 14 inches! If you wish to grow very long, straight carrots, get out there and double-dig the garden. Work up the soil at least two spades deep. Notice that I have not mentioned manures or composts. Carrots grow best in mineral or at least low-humus soils. In the home garden always plant carrots on soil that has not been manured or compost-dressed for at least twelve months. In the autumn double-dig the carrot section of the garden. In spring, dress the soil with 4 ounces of 5–10–5 fertilizer per square yard and fork or rotary till it as deeply as possible.

Planting

Open 1-inch-deep drills on 15-inch centers and sow three or four seeds per inch. With the carrot seeds in the drills, sprinkle in a few—very few—radish seeds as these will germinate quickly, breaking the soil crust for the fragile carrot seedlings, and also mark the rows of the slower-germinating carrots. Cover seeds to a depth of ¼ inch and pat down the soil with the back of a steel rake. Carrot seed germinates, depending on the strain, in six to fourteen days at a 60° F. soil temperature.

Cultivation and Management

For best results with carrots, never walk into the carrot bed from seeding to harvest as the compaction of your footsteps can cause carrots to go hairy, to grow crooked, or otherwise to misbehave. Rather, keep a couple of lengths of foot-wide plank handy and stand on these boards for all sowing, thinning, hoeing, and other management.

As soon as carrot seedlings have made three or four true leaves, thin them to stand 2 inches apart. Some gardeners wait to thin until young carrots are fountain-pen sized, useable in the kitchen, but this is risky business in all but the loosest, sandy soils. Also, get those radishes out of there within four weeks of germination as they cramp the carrots' style.

Carrots grow best in clean cultivation. Standing on the boards, cultivate carrot soil at least once each week. A Dutch scuffle hoe is the very best tool for the job, or use your steel-toothed garden rake. Thin the crop two times: first, while quite small, to a 2-inch spacing; then again in a few weeks, removing every other carrot for table use, for a final spacing of 4 inches. Unless your soil is loose, water the row an hour or so before thinning, and then water again to resettle disturbed plants. At harvest time pull carrots when the soil is wet, or better, with a narrow fork or spade, lift out the roots.

Pests and Diseases

Few pests and diseases damage the carrot crop. Most bothersome are the below-ground insects which bore into roots. Worst is carrot rust fly larvae—yellowish-white, legless grubs up to ⅓ inch long which tunnel into the outer flesh of carrot roots. The standard control always has been an application of 2 pounds of five percent chlordane dust per 1,000 square feet, raked into the top 6 inches of soil just before planting carrots. Unfortunately, the E.P.A. has banned this useful chemical without a hint of a successful alternate insecticide. Leafhoppers and aphids sometimes attack carrot foliage, but can be controlled with a malathion or diazinon spray or dust applied at weekly intervals.

Cultivars

In America three basic forms of carrots are grown, and all may be planted at one- to two-week intervals from very early spring right through late summer, though the Chantenay types are most successful where summers are hot and dry. The Gold Pak types—long, tapering carrots—are:

Imperator, 64 days; with a narrow shoulder, 9 to 10 inches long.

Ultra Pak, 63 days; extra-early, 10 inches long.

In addition, in carrot-growing areas, commercial growers use: **Gold Pak Improved, Gold Pak Elite, Gold Pak C69, Imperator Special No. 58, Imperator 408,** and more. All are supermarket-type carrots, highly bred for special carrot soil, worth growing.

The Nantes types of carrots are long with almost parallel sides, and blunt at the root tip.

Baby-finger Nantes, 50 days; a finger-sized European introduction to cook (or can) whole. Must be harvested while young and succulent.

Coreless Amsterdam, 55 days; easy to force; try it in a cold frame in fall or in late winter.

Scarlet Nantes, 65 days; coreless roots, very tender.

Touchon Deluxe, 58 days; a 7-inch root of superb flavor.

The Chantenay types of carrots are perhaps the least attractive of all, being slightly tapered, perhaps 6 inches long and 3 inches or more in thickness at the top. Despite their coarse appearance, when grown fast and harvested early they are delicious; they grow satisfactorily on dry, upland soils, and they make reasonable summer crops in hot climates.

Royal Chantenay, 60 days; deep, wedge-shaped; a good inland strain.

Red Cored Chantenay, 60 days; reddish-orange, stump-rooted and massive; tolerates heavy soil.

The newest hybrid carrots ought to be of special interest to home gardeners because they are among the best tasting. Not commonly offered by most mail-order seed houses or garden shops, look for these in catalogs of dealers who supply the truck garden industry.

Canuck, 64 days; a Stokes hybrid for northern muckland conditions.

Klondike Nantes, 56 days; a new European hybrid for northern gardens; sugary, superior flavor and color.

Spartan Sweet, 62 days; a very fine sort, long, tapered, well-colored and sweet.

Cauliflower

Brassica oleracea var. *botrytis*   Mustard family

Cauliflower is among the tastiest of the cabbage group of vegetables, but it is tricky to grow as it does not tolerate deep cold or hot weather. A maritime climate, such as that of the Pacific Northwest, suits it to perfection. However, where there is a will. . . . Once I knew a Midwesterner determined to grow good cauliflowers and he finally succeeded—by using deep cold frames and shooting for a very late fall or early winter crop. Today the short-term new hybrids enable all of us to grow cauliflower in early spring or in the fall.

Soil Preparation

Cauliflower grows well only on highly fertile but fairly tight soil. Before spading the cauliflower bed, dress it generously with manure or compost. The British spade in (believe it or not) either 20 pounds of barnyard manure or compost *per square yard*, or for the same area, 2 ounces of hoof and horn meal, plus 4 ounces of bonemeal, plus 1 ounce of potash! In the United States we add all the manure or compost that the budget will stand at spading, and let it go at that. Just prior to planting, rake in 4 ounces per square yard of an all-purpose fertilizer such as 10–10–10. If your soil is loose and well aerated, put in young cauliflower plants for best results.

Planting

For the spring crop, sow seedlings as early as possible—January in the South, a few weeks later in the north. I recommend starting seedlings in flats or pans from a proprietary seed germination mix under lights in the cool basement. Seed will germinate best at a warm room temperature, then move the container very close to bright lights and give the seedlings at least a sixteen-hour day. For your fall crop, start seedlings in mid-summer, growing them as cool as possible until the weather cools.

To move seedlings into the open garden, mark out rows on 24- to 30-inch centers, and set seedlings within the rows in similar spacings. For a spring crop you can push seedlings with side-dressings of ½ ounce per plant of nitrate of soda at three-week intervals. Hoe in the fertilizer and keep the soil reasonably moist. Do not over-force the fall crop as plants may become too soft and overly sensitive to frost. Rather, water them frequently with pale tea-colored manure water. Cauliflowers always are grown in clean cultivation; but where summer weather is hot, it is permissible to mulch with straw or hay between the rows to cool the soil.

Cultivation and Management

Hoe plants frequently but very shallowly, water often so the soil never dries. Fertilize as outlined above. The same insect pests that attack cabbage also parasitize cauliflower plants. As the leaves soon will be tied, it is important to keep young plants absolutely free of pests. Spray or dust often with Dylox while plants are young; after the leaves are tied to blanch the heads, dust weekly with a rotenone or pyrethrum preparation.

Watch the growing tip of the young plant closely. As soon as you can discern a button-like swelling, indicating "curd" formation, gently pull together all of the top foliage and tie it in a loose bunch with twine or a rubber band. Take care not to bruise or break the leaves. As soon as heads are large, and before the curd begins to "rice" and discolor, cut the stalk, trim the leaves, and use the vegetable as quickly as possible.

Cultivars

There is great confusion as to exactly what cauliflower is. In Europe there are spring and winter strains, quite different; in addition, there are green and purple varieties which may or may not be strange sorts of broccoli. In any case, in America most cauliflowers are of the spring and early summer persuasion, and some vegetable seed specialists also list the colored forms (which, incidentally, are not blanched by tying the leaves).

Early Snowball, 50 days; an open-pollinated sort, yielding snow-white heads of fine quality.

Snow Crown, 48 days; a closed-pollination hybrid; delicious 2-pound heads about 7½ inches in diameter.

(Most seed catalog sorts resemble one or the other of the above types).

The two colored forms available in this country, both even more delicious than white cauliflower and far better for home freezing, are *Early Purple Head,* 110 days; and *Chartreuse,* 115 days. Grow these as spring crops to finish up in early summer as they stand some heat.

Celeriac, Celery Root, Turnip-Rooted Celery

Apium graveolens var. *rapaceum*   Carrot Family

Celeriac is a close kin to celery botanically, in the garden, and on the table. The part eaten is the chunky, rather unlovely bottom portion. This is easier to grow than celery, and so far as cooking is concerned, makes a reasonable substitute. Gourmet recipes demand it. Celeriac is subject to the same insects and diseases common to celery.

Soil Preparation

Manure the soil generously in the autumn and spade very deeply. In spring, before forking, dress the area with 5–10–5 fertilizer, about 4 ounces per square yard. Celeriac is not too demanding, but good drainage combined with continuous soil moisture and full sunlight give best results. Nearly any good garden soil will do so long as it is well worked.

Planting

As for celery; start seedlings early, and transplant with care. These are not trenched, but grown on the level. Space seedlings every 12 inches in rows 18 inches apart. Take care not to set young plants deeper than they grew in the seedbed or in the pot. I always pot the seedlings three weeks before taking them to the open garden.

Cultivation and Management

Hoe frequently. Water sufficiently so soil never dries or overheats, but avoid soggy conditions. A light mulch of composted barnyard manure through hot summer weather is beneficial. Water every other week with tea-colored liquid manure or with a soluble fertilizer solution. Remove side growths as they appear. Some growers side-dress with nitrate of soda, ½ ounce per yard of row, once or twice during the season.

When heavy frosts are imminent, remove all but the center-most leaves of the plants and mulch deeply with loose straw. Where winters are comparatively mild, you may leave celeriac in the ground, digging roots as needed. Where winters are harsh, lift and store in a root cellar, or pare, dice, blanch, and freeze, or can, for later use.

Celery

Apium graveolens var. *dulce*   Carrot Family

Celery is an ancient vegetable, and one that is not at all easy to grow in less favored parts of the world. In the United States, celery areas include niches in California, Florida, Arizona, New York, New Jersey, Michigan, Ohio, Pennsylvania, and Washington. Black mucklands are the key to celery production. When labor was plentiful, most celery was grown to be blanched by covering the stems with soil some weeks before harvest. Today, while soil-blanched sorts still are widely favored for taste, texture, and flavor in home gardens of Europe and England, in America we settle for green or "self-blanched" celery from the supermarket. I think everyone ought to try a crop of celery and it ought to be grown for blanching. Once you taste the nutty-sweet, tender-crisp stalks of properly blanched celery, you will wonder how you ever tolerated the acrid stuff foisted off on us by the grocery stores!

Soil Preparation

The key to a good crop of celery is good soil preparation. If at all possible, start the autumn before planting time, or else get busy in early spring as soon as soil can be worked. Decide first whether to grow your crop in paired rows or in single rows.

For single rows (I recommend these for amateurs), mark out rows 3 feet apart (double rows go on 4-foot centers). Dig out a trench at least 18 inches deep and 12 inches wide (18 inches wide for double rows). Place the excavated soil in uniform mounds adjacent to both sides of the trench. A 6- to 8- inch layer of barely composted barnyard manure or rich compost goes into the trench to be treaded down. Rake in soil from the sides to cover the manure or compost, filling the trench to within 3 or 4 inches from the top. The trench should be prepared to this point some three to four weeks prior to planting time. If you grow certain European strains of celery for exhibition purposes (to impress the neighbors), you must fill the trench to the top as these strains resent trench culture but need the deep, enriched root run all the same.

Planting

In March, start seeds in flats or pans filled with a suitable germination substrate—I use either John Innes Germinating Compost and mix it in the basement or buy a proprietary preparation such as Redi-earth. Cover seeds to ¼-inch depth or less, and keep barely moist and at cool room temperature. Usually germination is complete in a week to ten days. When seedlings have three true leaves, prick off singly to small pots of suitable soil—I use the same medium the seed germinated in—and begin fertilizing with a half-strength liquid plant fertilizer such as Ra-Pid-Gro or Plant Miracle. If you are not set up for indoor gardening, wait to start seedlings just before the frost-free date and prepare a seedbed outdoors and proceed as above, transplanting and all. If you transplant into a bed, space seedlings 3 inches apart each way.

Grow seedlings fast by maintaining constant soil moisture; push with liquid manure applied every ten days. Put down slug poison bait at least once each week. When plants are 9 to 10 inches tall (early May through June), transplant seedlings to the prepared trench. This is a critical period. Water seedlings thoroughly before transplanting; bedded plants require two days of soaking, potted plants need thorough watering overnight. Set plants in at the same depth they were in the pots, not a bit deeper, or they will decay at the ground. Plant 9 to 12 inches apart, staggering seedlings in double rows.

Cultivation and Management

Keep plants free of slugs; push with liquid manure water at frequent intervals. Remove discolored or disease-spotted leaves as quickly as they appear. When young plants are 15 inches high, rake to pulverize soil on the trench mounds. Remove all side growth from the plants, then hold the leafy top of each plant with one hand and gently pull in soil from the mounds, drawing it well up around the *base* of the plants. Rake the soil to a uniform level in the now nearly filled trench after all plants are "earthed-up." In late summer a second earthing-up is in order; as before, pulverize the soil to make it easy to work with, and this time slip a wide, not too tight, rubber band around the top of each plant or tie loosely with raffia. As before, pull in soil to level the now-settled trench, but take care that the soil does not sift into the hearts of the plants. In October, earth-up the plants for a final blanching. As before, take care that soil does not sift into the plants as it will be deep this time, to the *lowest* leaves. Take care not to compress the soil against the plants. A good method for beginners is to use newspapers, stapling them into cylinders around each plant until earthing-up is complete (this time the soil will be quite mounded). Then slip out the paper collars. This allows soil to be stacked high up around the plants but keeps it from getting into the plant centers and prevents over-compaction. Blanched plants may be dug out anytime after ten days to two weeks, but longer blanching is beneficial so long as slugs are not a problem. Earthed-up plants may remain in the fall garden until quite heavy frosts threaten.

There are other ways to blanch celery—vertical boards may be mounted with stakes on both sides of the row of level-grown plants, and the space between filled with loose soil, taking care that earth does not get inside the plants, as mentioned above. Plants may even be blanched with black polyethylene plastic or paper wrap. But none of these methods yields the quality obtained by proper earthing-up in a trench.

Cultivars

In America a dozen or more strains of celery can be found by searching through seed catalogs. Try *Utah* or *Cornell 619* for your first attempt, and shoot for, perhaps, twenty-five plants in the garden. When you become more expert at celery growing and blanching, by all means write for English seed catalogs and try some of the superb British cultivars.

Among the commonest American strains are:

Beacon, 100 days; early, dark-green strain from Cornell, a short plant.

Cornell 619, 100 days; a fine-quality, self-blanching, golden-yellow strain that is improved by earthing-up.

Florida, 100 days; a very ribby relative of *Utah,* but with a very fine heart. Bushy and difficult to blanch.

Florimart, 105 days; deep medium-green, quite sweet, good for the home garden.

Golden Plume, 90 days; a self-blanching sort widely planted by commercial growers; soil-blanching improves it.

Tendercrisp, 105 days; a medium-height, medium-green cultivar with a large heart; good quality.

Utah, 100 days; the parent of several slow-bolting sorts such as *Slow Bolt* and *Non-Bolting Green No. 12,* both important commercial strains, as well as all of the Pascals, such as *Giant Pascal, Emerson Pascal, Summer Pascal, Fordhook,* and *Tendercrisp.* There are improved strains of *Utah,* such as *Utah 52–70* and *Improved Utah 52–70.* All are worth growing.

Celtuce, Chinese Lettuce

Latuca sativa   Composite Family

This strange plant made its appearance in an American seed catalog in the mid-1930's, with much-to-do about its versatility—young leaves usable as salad greens, stalks usable raw or cooked as celery substitutes. Actually, the plant is an upright-growing lettuce of the Romaine persuasion, with rather coarse, moderately palatable leaves and thickened stalks which are edible—not delicious, but edible. This, in my estimation, is purely a novelty, not a vegetable to be taken seriously.

Soil Preparation

Any good garden loam, well-manured or compost-enriched and fertilized with 4 or 5 ounces per square yard of 10–6–4, will produce a vigorous crop of celtuce. The plant demands full sun and fast drainage. It fails in dry soil and wilts in wind and hot weather. Grow it as a spring crop.

Planting

Seed this where it is to grow. Mark off rows on 18-inch centers in early spring; open drills 1 inch deep and sow seeds one or two to the inch. As young plants reach usable size, thin for salads. By the time young plants are 6 to 7 inches tall they should stand about 15 inches apart.

Cultivation and Management

Hoe celtuce plants often to keep soil loose and weed-free. When dry, water thoroughly. If plants are off-color or slow, drench soil near the roots with manure water. Once spacing is complete, a 2-inch layer of coarse, rather raw compost helps insulate soil against summer sun.

With plants fully spaced you can remove lower leaves for salads or for cooking before they go tough and leathery. Before the top tuft of leaves deteriorates, harvest the thickened stalk for table use. In my experience, celtuce is an ideal crop for supplying greens for the chicken coop—the birds shred the leaves and stems in no time and soon egg yolks take on a deeper golden color.

Almost no pests or serious diseases affect celtuce.

Chard, Swiss Chard

Beta vulgaris var. *cicla*   Goosefoot Family

The chards are beets without swollen roots, grown for the leafy tops which are cooked as "greens." They may be used in place of spinach in the summer garden as they can withstand considerable heat.

Soil Preparation

As for beets; deeply worked, relatively high-humus, fertile soil will give the best crops. As the vegetable is leafy, apply at least 5 ounces per square yard of 5–10–5 fertilizer to the soil and fork this in just prior to seed planting.

Planting

For mid-spring through early summer, open 1-inch-deep drills on 15- to 18-inch centers. Sow two or three seeds per inch, cover with ½ inch soil, and pat down the row with the back of a steel garden rake. Seedlings appear in a week to ten days if the soil is moist at planting time.

Cultivation and Management

Cultivate the chard rows as soon as the seed germinates; the easiest way is to drag a common garden rake through the soil every few days so weed seedlings are dislodged and the soil is kept loose on top. When seedlings are 4 inches high, thin to stand 4 inches apart; when they begin to crowd, thin again—by now the vegetable should be large enough to eat. Ultimate spacing for long-standing plants is 12 inches. Never allow the soil to go completely dry. At three-week intervals, wide-dress on both sides of the row with nitrate of soda (2 ounces per yard of row), or water generously with tea-colored manure water. From the more mature, well-spaced plants, harvest only the outer leaves, allowing the plants to stand for quite a long time.

Pests and Diseases

Pests and diseases of the chards are the same as for beets. Watch especially for blister beetles in mid-summer as they can quickly defoliate the plants. Fortunately, most garden insecticide dusts give good control.

Chicory

Cichorium intybus   Composite Family

Chicory is a close relative of the endives,*Cichorium endivia* selections. Despite the close kinship of the plants botanically, as vegetables they are miles apart in usage and culture, and therefore are treated separately here. Common chicory is a familiar roadside weed throughout most of the northern hemisphere. Because of its blue, pink, or white flowers which open every sunny dawn, the plant has found its way into perennial beds and borders in Europe and America. Folks who enjoy a mess of spring greens often seek out wild chicory plants and add a few leaves to their collection. Tender young leaves are eaten cooked, spinach-fashion, or wilted in a salad. The roots may be washed and dried, to be ground for chicory coffee. Among cultivated sorts, the leafy ones do not produce usable roots, and the heavy rooted sorts are not usually well regarded for their leafy tops.

Soil Preparation

The chicories grow in any well-prepared garden soil. Best production is on soil manured heavily the year before for another crop, and top-dressed with 2 to 4 ounces of 5–10–5 fertilizer per square yard before spading in the spring. All chicories are grown in a clean cultivation. Usually no additional fertilizer is added through the growing season.

Planting

The various sorts of chicory are treated differently. Plant the Italian strains (Italian dandelion) in early fall or early spring and harvest young leaves in late spring while they are still tender. Plant seed of the "French endive," a strain usually identified as witloof chicory, in late spring or early summer in very deeply worked soil (to produce deep, strong roots). Grow these throughout summer in clean cultivation. The roots will be used indoors in winter to produce the leafy buds known as witloof chicory.

Both sorts of chicory are seeded directly where they are to grow. Mark out drills as close as one foot and open them to a depth of 1½ inches. Sow seeds sparsely, two or three per inch. Cover with not more than ½ inch of soil. Seeds germinate in a week to ten days. Thin Italian dandelion sorts to stand 12 inches apart. Witloof chicory plants may be grown as close together as 9 inches.

Cultivation and Management

Cultivate all sorts of chicory frequently. The use of any sort of organic mulch invites slugs which soon riddle leaves and tender shoots. Water frequently when plants are young so soil never completely dries. It is possible to maintain plants of the Italian dandelion strains for several years if bloom shoots are removed as they appear. But this ties up a garden row throughout the year—interfering with crop rotation, plowing or spading, and all the rest—for just a short spring harvest. I suggest planting fresh each year. Harvest leaves of the Italian dandelion sorts while they are sweet and not too bitter; when hot weather sets in, toss the plants on the compost pile and plant a few hills of summer squash or another summer vegetable.

You have to leave roots of the witloof chicory in place throughout the summer. Keep plants growing steadily with plenty of water. If leaves are thin or pale, apply tea-colored liquid manure water or a foliar fertilizer. In late fall, with a deep spade lift the roots, taking care not to break them. Select the best ones—those with crowns at least 2 inches across (but not much larger) and about 12 inches long. With a sharp knife, trim away leaves and side-shoots. Let the crowns air-dry (roots covered with loose soil) for a day or two. Store the roots in a cool, dry, dark place (the root cellar, the cold garage, or in a box buried below frost line in the garden). After January 10, every two weeks plant a few roots 2 or 3 inches apart in deep boxes of sifted compost or fine sand, leaving the crowns exposed about an inch. Cover each planted box with another inverted box. Keep the planted box soil moderately moist, but never wet, and hold at about 50° F. for four to six weeks until tight buds have formed which resemble heads of Romaine lettuce. Cut these with a bit of the crown and use for braising, salads, or for other culinary purposes. When roots no longer produce buds, discard them.

Pests and Diseases

Almost no pests or diseases bother chicories. If snails and slugs are a problem, use slug bait as directed by the manufacturer (be sure witloof chicory roots are completely free of these pests before storing). Occasionally grasshoppers attack garden plants; a suitable bait or spray should be applied.

Cultivars

Witloof Chicory, 110 days; the various "improved" strains of this vegetable are all similar, some force easier than others. Use this cultivar only for forcing.

Among the leafy chicory sorts known as a group as "Italian Dandelion" are:

Cicoria Catalogna (Radichetta), 65 days; with foot-long, dark-green leaves, deeply notched. Both leaves and tender stalks are used.

Cicoria San Pasquale, 70 days; this is a very tender, exceptionally leafy strain used for Italian salads.

Magdeburgh (Cicoria Siciliana), 100 days; this probably is the true "Italian dandelion" which is grown for blanching, for cooked greens, and especially, for Italian salads. The roots of this sort may be lifted, scrubbed, dried, and ground for a coffee substitute.

Chinese Cabbage or Celery Cabbage

Brassica pekinensis and *B. chinensis*　　　Mustard Family

Chinese cabbages recently have sprung into great prominence throughout the western world as people find stir-fried Oriental cooking to their taste and as truck gardeners find how easy it is to produce a tremendous crop of Chinese cabbage per acre. Throughout Europe, especially in Germany, and in the United States, Chinese cabbages are becoming important crops. They are ideal for home growing as a great volume can be produced on a small space. The trick is to use the newest hybrid sorts. These are graded to the seasons. For success, you must plant according to schedule. All types of Chinese cabbages may be used fresh as salad vegetables or cooked.

Soil Preparation

As for other cabbages, Chinese cabbages do best on soil that has been manured heavily or compost-enriched in the fall, with 30 to 40 pounds per 1,000 square feet of a balanced fertilizer (as 5–10–5) forked under in the spring.

Planting

With the older sorts, both Pak-Choi and Pe-tsai types, it was essential to sow seeds in the spring as soon as soil was workable in order to get at least a partial crop before warm weather brought the plants to the bolting (seed-stalk producing) stage. Today, with the Pak-Choi (the Wong Bok commercial types) we select seed of strains intended either for spring, summer, or fall culture. Seed houses invariably recommend only direct sowing of these. But I have started seeds in flats of Redi-earth, transplanted the seedlings individually into pots, and transplanted these to the garden with great success. Needless to say, direct sowing is simpler, though more seed is required. Mark out rows on 18-inch centers and set seedlings 18 inches apart in the rows, or open drills 1½ inches deep, sow seeds two or three to the inch, and thin to stand 12 to 15 inches apart. The so-called "hybrid" sorts make shorter, wider plants, and these need more room than the Chihli sorts.

Cultivation and Management

Keep Chinese cabbage in clean cultivation; soil always should be moderately moist, never completely dry under any circumstances. Side-dress seedlings with ½ ounce of nitrate of soda per yard of row; repeat the application when plants are half-grown. These respond exceptionally well to frequent waterings with tea-colored manure water. Hoe frequently. For late spring and for the summer crops mulch deeply with straw between the rows to help cool the soil; but do not crowd mulch up to the plants.

Pests and Diseases

Few diseases attack Chinese cabbages though occasionally leaf spots may develop on the outer foliage. Insect pests may be formidable, including the various cabbage worms, flea beetles, and harlequin plant bugs. Apply rotenone, pyrethrum, or Dylox to young plants; at least three weeks before harvest use only rotenone, pyrethrum, or diazinon.

Cultivars

Pe-tsai, 75 days; a varied group of non-heading cultivars. Seed of these is difficult to find outside favored locations such as the San Francisco area.

Among the Pak-Choi types (the commercial Wong Boks) are:
Chihli, now superseded by the much better
Michihli, 78 days; a tall, cylindrical head to 18 inches, 4 inches in diameter, crisp and tender. Does not store well.

The fine hybrids of this group, really the only thing for home growing, are:
Springtime, 60 days; with a short, thick head to 3½ pounds; suitable only for earliest spring planting as it bolts with heat. Makes a fall crop, too, and stores well.
Summertime, 70 days; plant in July for an early fall harvest; heads 6 to 8 pounds, 10 inches high. Good for storing, not too good where late summer temperatures rise above 85° F.
Wintertime, 80 days; start these in late July or early August where summers are hot and autumns are long; 7- to 9-pound heads, well-filled and firm; stores well. This one is my main crop.

The three hybrids listed above will hold in the vegetable bin of your refrigerator for three to six months if put away clean!

Sweet Corn

Zea mays var. *Rugosa*   Grass Family

Sweet corn is the supreme home garden product because it is at its delicious best when gathered, cooked, and eaten all within an hour. As sweet corn lends itself to concentrated production, even a small patch, properly handled, can supply the average family with several Lucullan meals. And the stalks are a marvelous additive, freshly chopped, for the compost pile, or they may be spaded directly into the garden soil. Like all grasses, sweet corn will grow on almost any soil (though well-drained, rather heavy loam soils give the best results) provided sufficient manures and fertilizer are added. If your property has a sunny area, by all means, plant several rotations of sweet corn; your girth may suffer but your meals will be memorable.

Soil Preparation

In the fall, turn sweet corn soil as deeply as possible, working in great quantities of barnyard manure or compost mixed three parts to one of dehydrated manure—three bushels per 100 square feet should be the minimum. The more the humus-yielding organic matter, the finer the crop of corn Before the ground is forked up in the spring for seeding, top-dress with 5–10–10 fertilizer at 3 to 4 pounds per 100 square feet (you can use 6–10–4 fertilizer on older, top-quality garden soil). If you were unable to spade in the manure or compost, add another pound of fertilizer per 100 square feet. Fork the soil twice as sweet corn does best in soil that is completely uniform. Here is where the rotary tiller can earn its keep.

Planting

Sweet corn always is grown from seed and in much of the country by directly sown seed. In less-favored climates, home gardeners have to resort to potted corn plants, bought at market, to be set like tomato plants! How strange this sounds to Midwestern gardeners. There are two basic patterns for growing sweet corn. One is the row pattern, where at least three rows (better four or five) of corn are planted at the same time, side by side. The other is the "hill" pattern, with three to six plants closely grouped to make a "hill," and the hills are in three or more rows. The whole point of grouping corn plants is for efficient pollination. In order for kernels to develop on the corn ears, every kernel must receive a grain of pollen on its strand of corn silk, the pollen falling from the tassels above. When corn is planted in blocks, either in rows or hills, the set of kernels is satisfactory, but often single-row plantings yield only partially filled ears because breezes blow the pollen away.

To plant corn, wait until the soil begins to warm and the danger of frost is past. I always plant a risk crop some ten or fifteen days before the frost-free date, and only once have I lost a crop to unseasonable weather. The early corn is worth the risk. For planting in rows, mark them out on 30- to 36-inch centers. Open the drills with a Warren hoe (heart-shaped) or with the corner of a conventional hoe to a depth of 4 to 6 inches. In spring and early summer usually the soil is moist enough to insure quick, uniform germination. But in summer it is a good idea to flood the furrows once or twice before sowing seed, then sow seed on the mud and cover with dry soil. Sow corn kernels 3 to 4 inches apart in the row. Cover with about ¾ inch of soil and tread down to compact or tamp with the back of a rake. Germination occurs in four to eight days, depending on soil temperature. As seedlings reach the three- or four-leaf stage, pull in soil to fill the furrows.

To plant corn in hills, mark off rows on 36-inch centers and go down each row with a yardstick and hoe making a mark every 36 inches. At each mark, hoe open a dinner plate-sized patch 3 or 4 inches deep and scatter in six or eight corn kernels at least 3 inches apart. Cover with soil and tread down.

Cultivation and Management

Thinning is your first job, and how painful it is to pull up those bright green little seedlings. In rows, thin first to 6-inch intervals; in the hills, thin to about eight well-spaced plants per hill. At thinning time (when seedlings are 6 to 8 inches tall), broadcast a band of ammonium nitrate or nitrate of soda along each side of the row or in a broad band around each hill; cultivate this into the soil. One measuring cupful of fertilizer per yard is about right.

Keep sweet corn in clean cultivation, at least until very hot mid-summer. Water it thoroughly any week when natural rainfall is less than one inch. The best way to water corn is with a canvas soil soaker, but overhead irrigation is better than no watering at all. Never allow the soil to crust and bake. When young plants are nearing knee-high, thin again. Plants should stand 10 to 12 inches apart in rows, or leave three to six plants per hill. If plants are strong, sturdy, and dark green, leave more of them. Fertilize as before. When the tassels show from their sheaths, fertilize again, as before, for the last time. From now on, never allow the plants to suffer from water shortage. At least an inch of water per week is essential. With a mid-summer crop, at tasseling time you may choose to put down a deep straw mulch to help hold soil moisture.

Pests and Diseases

Any number of insect pests and several diseases may attack sweet corn. Your first line of defense is to buy treated seed. Usually the chemical is tinted, so do not be surprised to find yourself with bright pink seed corn. Mercurials were and are among the best seed treatment chemicals but were banned by the government and Captan now usually is substituted. These chemicals are functional in two ways: they help reduce loss of seed from decay in the soil and they prevent smut spores from being carried into the garden on the seed.

One of the more than twenty insect pests of corn, corn earworm and the two corn borers are the worst. Earworms (stout, striped larvae) feed on the silk and the kernels at the tips of the ears. Spray or dust silks as soon as they emerge with Sevin and repeat the application at three-day intervals. Corn borers attack the corn stalks, ruining the entire plant for ear production; they also bore into ears. When young stalks are about 18 inches high, with a funnel of furled leaves at the top, begin treating with Sevin or rotenone or pyrethrum and continue treatment at two-week intervals. Normally, I do not recommend Sevin because in my experience a secondary result of its use is an infestation of spider mites brought on, no doubt, by their predators having been killed by the insecticide. Also, it kills all of the honeybees that come for the corn pollen. But Sevin does give clean corn ears.

Corn flea beetles, army worms, and similar pests usually are controlled by the insecticides applied for earworms and stalk borers, but if they persist, apply Dylox or diazinon.

Cultivars

Dozens of strains of sweet corn are available and most are pretty good though quality and productivity varies between strains in different parts of the country. By all means, select a cultivar recommended for your area. I cannot bring myself to recommend the so-called miniature and dwarf strains. These small plants take up almost as much space as the full-sized corn plants, and their ears are ridiculously tiny. What does it matter whether your corn plants are 4 feet or 7 feet high?

Early Cultivars
Extra Early Super Sweet, 67 days; sweet as **Illinichief.**
Golden Beauty, 64 days; a favorite, adaptable, early sort.
Royal Crest, 64 days; similar to the older **Earliking,** but more disease resistant.

Main Crop Cultivars
Gold Cup, 80 days; fine-quality ears on moderate-sized plants.
Golden Cross Bantam, 80 days; with the quality of disease-susceptible **Golden Bantam,** but more vigorous, and disease resistant.
Golden Jubilee, 84 days; large ears, sugary, good for freezing.
Illinichief, 87 days; unusual in that it has almost twice the sugar content of other sweet corns; delicious, but grow no other corn in the garden as cross-pollination gives tasteless results.
Improved Carmelcross, 70 days; long, well-filled ears, a fine freezer sort.
Iochief Hybrid, 83 days; a favorite hybrid for the Midwest.
Northern Belle, 74 days; small kernels on long, slender cobs, exceptionally fine flavor.
Tri-gold, 84 days; one of the finest truck garden strains, and a good home garden sort.
Wonderful, 78 days; irregular rows of kernels on long cobs; superb flavor. This is my main table and freezer corn.

Many other fine strains of sweet corn are available, including brand-new "double sugar" hybrids without the pollination drawbacks of **Illinichief.** As these become available, try a test planting.

Cress, Garden
(Upland Cress, Peppergrass)

Lepidium sativum   Mustard Family

The English couldn't make it through tea without cress sprouts to scatter on and in their tea sandwiches. Here is the ideal windowsill crop, and something for the children to grow in mid-winter. About ten days elapse between sowing and harvest because the tiny seedlings are clipped for use when the seed-leaves are fully expanded. Cress sprouts are pungent, delicious, and laden with vitamins. Everyone ought to grow cress throughout the winter. If you don't have afternoon tea, sprinkle the sprouts on salads, cold or warm meats, or use to garnish meat and vegetable dishes.

Soil Preparation

Cress usually is not grown in soil but in a container of a neutral medium which serves only to hold moisture. One method is to line a bowl or basket with several layers of clean cheesecloth, burlap, or unbleached muslin; paper towels work too, if kept constantly moist.

Planting

Sprinkle cress seeds thickly (one layer only) over the damp fabric or paper and cover with a clean plate or with a piece of opaque paper. Seeds germinate in a few days and need full sunlight immediately.

Cultivation and Management

There is no cultivation of this brief crop. Grow sprouted seedlings in your chilliest windowsill in brightest light. When seed-leaves are fully expanded, before true leaves appear, shear off the seedlings with a small scissors. Then freshen sprouts in chilled water, drain, and they are ready for use.

Tea sandwich experts like to mix equal parts of upland cress and watercress sprouts for gourmet eating. To get them to the harvesting point together, sow upland cress seeds three or four days after the watercress.

Cucumber

Cucumis sativus   Cucumber Family

Cucumbers are an ancient crop; at the time of Christ they were a favorite breakfast item in Palestine! Until recently, growers grew either white-spined cucumbers for table use (these are the large, dark-green ones found in supermarkets) or the paler, black-spined ones for pickling. Today modern hybridizing has blurred the distinction, but pickle-makers are tending toward darker colored cucumbers for pickles. Also, the far more delicate Chinese and European table strains are coming into common culture; the former are easy outdoors on any fence or trellis, the latter almost exclusively suited for forced indoor culture.

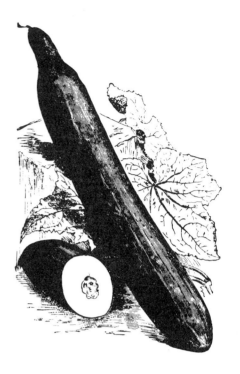

Soil Preparation

Cucumbers are heavy feeders, thriving in a high-organic-content soil or in heavily enriched sandy loam. They germinate and grow successfully only when the soil is thoroughly warmed, so early sowing is a waste. In the open garden, mark out hills on a 4 × 4-foot grid; broadcast and till in 5–10–10 fertilizer over the cucumber patch, 35 pounds per 1,000 square feet, and heap a shovelful of well-rotted barnyard manure or enriched compost at each hill; sow seed 3 or 4 per hill. For rows: alternatively strew fertilizer and manure along each row and turn it under; sow seed for a final spacing of 6 to 8 inches. Plants should be allowed to run, they will grow and produce even better on a temporary trellis or stretched fencing. If you are lacking space, by all means, grow your cucumbers upright. The Chinese and Japanese hybrids produce well only when grown on a trellis. Another way to save space is to plant cucumbers on the compost pile; if well-fertilized they do extra well here, serve to camouflage the heap, and free garden space for another crop.

Planting

When night air temperature remains above 60° F., plant cucumber seeds on dampened soil, cover with ½ inch of fine soil, lightly compacted. Alternatively, fill 3-inch pots with a good germinating mix, plant two seeds per pot three to five weeks before your last average frost-free date, and set seedlings into the garden when soil is warm.

Cultivation and Management

Always keep young cucumbers in clean cultivation; if you are in a high humidity area, better keep them clean throughout summer as mulch holds moisture and aggravates a mildew condition, but where air is relatively dry, apply a loose straw mulch to grown cucumbers before the plants begin to sprawl. When young plants have four or five leaves, dress each hill (or yard of row) with 4 ounces of nitrate of soda or with 2 ounces of ammonium nitrate; keep this solution 6 inches from the plants and scratch into the soil, then water. Never allow cucumber plants to wilt badly for want of water, but apply water in early morning, to the soil only, if possible. Cucumber plants growing on a compost heap need liquid fertilizer applications at bi-weekly intervals, unless the compost is greatly enriched. Experienced gardeners often set hilled cucumbers around a sunken, perforated 3-pound coffee can partially filled with fresh barnyard manure. The can is water-filled daily to maintain high soil moisture and a steady flow of organic nutrients to the plants.

Pests and Diseases

Both striped and spotted cucumber beetles feed on leaves and blossoms of young plants, and their larvae gnaw on stems and roots causing even more extensive damage. Clean up all garden debris annually as these pests overwinter as adults in such waste matter. Fall spade the garden to further reduce them, and spray or dust with methoxychlor, Dylox, or rotenone or pyrethrum at frequent intervals when insects first appear. Melon aphids sometimes are a pest and will be controlled by malathion, diazinon, or a nicotine-sulfate spray. Pickle worms sometimes eat into blossoms, buds, and cucumbers in late summer; the controls recommended for beetles will destroy these. Occasionally squash bugs move into cucumbers; spray or dust leaves and stems from below with malathion.

To avoid the several leaf diseases and viruses, plant resistant or tolerant strains. Insect control does much to reduce the spread of several destructive diseases, particularly bacterial wilt, which cannot be combated directly. For most leaf diseases apply zineb or manzate when the first signs of infection appear or when weather is unfavorable.

Cultivars

Today dozens upon dozens of superior strains are

available to the homeowner. To choose sensibly, first define your use. For strictly table eating, try the trellis strains from the Orient such as *China, Japanese Long Picking,* and, of all things, *'Burpless Hybrid,'* the latter being one of the easiest and best despite its title. For general table use and perhaps for dill pickles try the following:

Long Marketer, 60 days; long, slim, good color.

Marketer, 60 days; an old standard variety, very popular; similar to the above, but thicker.

Marketmore, 55 days; a very fine early slicer, tolerant of scab and mosaic.

Patio Pick, 48 days; an ideal home sort as it is suitable for table use but also is good for pickling. Tolerates scab, powdery mildew, and downy mildew.

Sweet Slice, 62 days; a standard type but bitter-free and "burpless" with considerable disease tolerance. Highly recommended.

Among the better pickling strains are:

National Pickling, 52 days; a fine old strain but superseded by newer sorts.

Pioneer, 51 days; a gynecious hybrid (produces female blooms only) blended with a few seeds of a male pollinator; resists or tolerates most diseases. Very fine.

Salty, 53 days; a white spine gynecious hybrid tolerant to many diseases. With good shape and deep-green color, this is very popular.

Dandelion

Taraxacum officinale   Composite Family

Most gardeners have sufficient dandelions without planting more; but for those who like lots of greens, there is a thick-leaved strain which may be bleached under a flat tile or bunched and tied as endive, giving a white-hearted, leafy vegetable that is only slightly bitter. Dandelion is a perennial and the roots are regenerative. If you plant it in your garden for greens, take care that it does not go to seed, and when you are through with it, fork out the roots without breaking them (pieces left in the soil will start new plants) and air-dry them to be sure they are killed.

Soil Preparation

While dandelions will grow in any soil, for best leaves, plant in deeply spaded, heavily manured or compost-enriched soil built up with 5 ounces of 10–10–10 fertilizer per square yard just before planting.

Planting

In mid-spring, rake down the row so soil is fine and draw open a drill not more than ½ inch deep, shallower is better. Scatter seeds, one or two per inch, and cover with not more than ¼ inch of fine soil. Pat down firmly with the back of the rake. In milder climates, you can sow dandelion seed in early fall for a very early spring crop.

Cultivation and Management

Keep dandelions in clean cultivation; as plants grow, thin to stand 4 inches apart. Push with liquid fertilizer (liquid manure is ideal) and ample water. Pinch out flower buds as they appear deep in the crown, and when a good rosette has formed, pull together the leaves and tie them at the tip so the heart will blanch in two or three weeks. When you harvest a plant, destroy the root.

Dandelions are remarkably free from pests and diseases.

Cultivars

Thick-Leaved, 95 days; vigorous, quick-growing, with extra-thick leaves; best when blanched.

Eggplant (Aubergine)

Solanum melongena var. *esculentum*
(in Europe, var. *ovigerum*)   Nightshade Family

The eggplant is a favorite in the Middle East, Turkey and Greece, and is fairly common elsewhere. It is a relative of the tomato, pepper, and the deadly nightshade. This truly is a tropical plant; it tolerates no chill, no stoppage in growth. The secret to these is to start them under heat and bring them on fast, transplanting frequently till they go to the open garden when soil is warm, and then push them with liquid manure or with a very diluted liquid fertilizer solution. If you can fend off solanaceous diseases and flea beetles you will reap quite a lot of fruit.

Soil Preparation

Select a place where tomatoes and peppers have not grown for several years and where you have had no nematode troubles. Soil should be very deeply dug with 20 pounds or more of barnyard manure in fall or very early spring, or substitute with a mixture of compost and dehydrated manure. Sandy or silt loams give best results as they heat better than heavier soils. Prior to setting plants, dress and rake in 5 ounces of 5–10–5 fertilizer per square yard.

Planting

Start seeds indoors six to eight weeks before the frost-free date in any suitable germinating compost with bottom heat at 80° to 85° F. Seed will germinate in five to ten days. Grow seedlings at 70° to 75° F. with very bright light, and keep fairly damp. Add a very diluted fertilizer solution to the water each week; if plants slow down, move them to larger pots. When nighttime temperature holds above 50° F. you can go to the open garden with your plants; harden them by reducing water for four to five days. Set plants 24 inches apart in rows on 30- to 36-inch centers.

Cultivation and Management

Four critical aspects of eggplant culture have to be managed; cultivation, fertilization, watering, and disease and insect control. Meet the needs and you will have eggplant fruit galore. Water-in newly set plants with a highly soluble phosphate transplant fertilizer. Thereafter, the best way to fertilize is with tea-colored manure water applied to damp soil once each week; otherwise, side-dress with nitrate of soda, 1 to 2 ounces per running yard, on both sides of the plants two or three times through the summer. Water your eggplants sufficiently often so the soil will never be dry ½ inch below the surface. It is tempting to mulch them, but except in the hottest climates mulching is a bad idea as the roots need sun-heated soil. Hoe very shallowly—a scuffle hoe is best—once each week.

Pests and Diseases

Immediately initiate a weekly dusting or spraying program; the main pest is flea-beetle, but aphids, Colorado potato beetle, leafhoppers, and other pests may also show up. Diazinon will do the job. Sevin is all right if no one for a few miles around keeps honeybees. Repeat insect control every week. There is no easy way to combat fungus diseases as these are soil-borne; just avoid soil where eggplant relatives have grown recently.

Cultivars

Black Beauty (including *Imperial Black Beauty*), 75 days; among the largest of the purple-black fruited sorts, plants to 18 inches.
Black Magic, 73 days; fruit dark purple, deep oval, medium-sized. Plants are vigorous.
Burpee Hybrid, 70 days; fruit oval, deep purple, medium-sized. Plants are tall and semi-spreading.
Classic, 75 days; purple-black, long, tapered fruit. Plant is rather erect. Choice.
Dusky, 56 days; fruit black-skinned, cylindrical, small. Plants small. Home garden type.
Early Hybrid, 65 days; purple, pear-shaped; resists fusarium wilt. Heavy yields.
Jersey King, 75 days; fruit dark purple, cylindrical, 10 by 4½ inches, better when harvested at a smaller size. Strong plants.

The white and other-colored eggplants are novelties scarcely worth growing.

Garbanzos, Chick-Peas

Cicer arietinum   Legume Family

Garbanzos are popular in India, southern Europe, and some Near Eastern countries. The Mexicans also have adopted them as a high-protein food. Americans are learning to know them as salad ingredients and as a puree base for dips. These are neither peas nor beans, but legume relatives.

Soil Preparation

Plant garbanzos in moderately fertile, loose loam that is very well drained. For best results, select a planting area that was heavily manured a year earlier for a crop of heavy nutrient plants such as potatoes, eggplants, or melons. In the spring, dress the soil with 4 ounces per square yard of a mixture of three parts superphosphate and one part potash (muriate of potassium). These bushy plants grow best in absolutely clean cultivation.

Planting

When danger of frost is past and the soil is warm to the touch, fork it up to loosen and draw open 3-inch-deep drills in rows on 20- to 30-inch centers. Plant garbanzos four or five inches apart, and cover to a depth of 1½ inches. Walk down the soil-covered rows to press seeds firmly into the soil. When young plants have several leaves, thin to stand 10 to 12 inches apart.

Cultivation and Management

Garbanzos grow into bushy plants with one or two seeds in an inflated pod. Pods will completely cover the stems of well-grown plants. Cultivate plants frequently but shallowly as roots are just under the surface. If no rain falls for ten days, irrigate deeply using a shallow trench midway between adjacent rows, or better, use a canvas soil soaker. Allow the soil to dry to a depth of an inch or so before watering again. Garbanzos seldom require additional fertilizer, but if a crop is faltering with the plants puny and yellowish, try an application of a water-soluble foliar fertilizer applied as a spray.

As wrinkled, ball-shaped seeds develop in the pods, pick

and shell out to eat freshly cooked. Or allow the pods to yellow and become almost dry, then pick and finish drying on newspapers in a warm, dry place; shell out the garbanzos to be further dried, then store in a metal or glass container.

Pests and Diseases

Few pests bother these sturdy plants; however, bean beetles, bean weevils, and aphids all may be pests. As these appear spray or dust with malathion, a rotenone or pyrethrum preparation, diazinon, or apply an all-purpose vegetable garden insecticide, carefully following instructions on the container.

Garlic

Allium sativum   Lily Family

Garlic is another ancient vegetable; it grows best in mild north temperate conditions but can be grown in the cooler areas. For details of soil preparation, cultivation and management, *see* Onion.

Planting

Garlic grows from "cloves" only, these being the segments of the bulb after the papery enclosing membrane is removed. Where the climate is mild, Zone V and southward, set cloves in mid- to late summer; where winters are rather severe, plant cloves in spring when soil is somewhat warmed and workable. Deep planting is required for best results; open a trench in properly fertilized and prepared soil. Set cloves 4 inches apart and cover with 2 inches of pulverized soil; compact lightly. As leaves show above ground, proceed as for onions.

Harvest garlic when the tops bend over and leaves begin to die.

Horseradish

Armoracia lapathifolia   Mustard Family

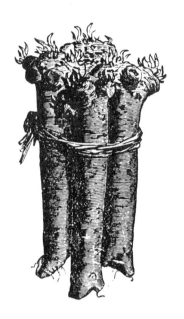

This coarse-leaved, large perennial plant is grown mainly for its pungent, parsnip-like roots which are grated to make a condiment, but some gardeners, when collecting boiling greens in the spring, add a few tender young horseradish leaves to the mixture for additional flavor. This really is not a plant for the vegetable garden as it stands the year yound, interfering with cultivation, tilling, and all the rest. If you wish to grow it, shove it into the perennial border where a mass of bold, vertical foliage is needed, or tuck it in an out-of-the-way corner of the service yard.

Soil Preparation

For thick, straight roots, spade the horseradish bed to a depth of 18 inches or more and add as much as one-third volume of old barnyard manure or compost. Two or three weeks before planting, dress the bed with 5 ounces per square yard of bone-meal or 2 ounces of superphosphate, and fork in deeply.

Planting

The best plants are raised from 6- to 8-inch-long finger-thick pieces of root planted almost vertically in early spring, with the upper end of the root about an inch below the soil surface, deeper in light soil. Space plants 18 inches apart. Three or four plants are more than enough for the average family.

Cultivation and Management

Keep horseradish plants in clean cultivation and keep them growing strongly by fertilizing every two or three weeks with a very light dusting of 5–10–5 fertilizer, or water with dilute manure water. Never allow plants to suffer from drought; water deeply during dry periods.

Harvest horseradish in the fall before the tops freeze. With a long fork or a sharpshooter, lift the clump; take care not to break up the root system. Shake off the soil, cut back the tops for compost, and wash the roots clean. Save the large ones to grind for prepared horseradish; the smaller ones are trimmed for replanting. Make a straight horizontal cut at the upper end and a slanting cut at the bottom. That way you can tell top from bottom at replanting time. Home growers prefer to replant right away in reworked soil, mulching the bed deeply with straw or hay over winter. Others prefer to hold the propagation roots in a box of barely damp sand in a chilly cellar or garage (just above freezing).

Pests and Diseases

Several insects gnaw on horseradish leaves; the worst pest is the tiny jumping flea beetle which should be controlled with Dylox, diazinon, or methoxychlor. Keep after this pest as he will multiply and attack many other plants in the garden even though he does no severe damage to the horseradish.

Cultivars

Bohemian, 150 days; roots are large, white, hot and sweet. This is the best.

Kale

Brassica oleracea var. *acephala*   Cabbage Family
and *B. napa*

Kales are ancient vegetables; those originating from *Brassica oleracea* var. *acephala* are the Scotch and curled kales, while the Siberian kales originate from *B. napa,* according to British authorities. Presumably the other cabbage relatives originated from these primitive forms. Kales are eaten as leafy vegetables; they are rather harsh, sometimes stringy, but if gathered fresh and young may be quite palatable. Their greatest merit is their ability to stand well into the winter, all winter in the South.

Soil Preparation

Work up soil for kale well in advance to planting so it can settle down again, or else plant it where a manured and fertilized crop, such as onions, has grown. Never plant where a cabbage relative has grown within the past season because of disease problems. On unprepared ground, spread 2 bushels per 100 square feet of barnyard manure or compost, and dress with 2½ pounds of 5–10–5 fertilizer. Work these through the soil and walk down the soil to make it compact.

Planting

Sow seed sparsely in rows on 2-foot centers, then thin plants to 2 feet apart; or, better, start seedlings in a seedbed or in flats (in the North), then set plants. Dwarf varieties may go 18 inches apart. In the North, start seeds as for cabbage, in very early spring and again in early August. In the South, sow seed from mid-August to mid-October for all winter crops.

Cultivation and Management

To cut down on insect pests and disease, keep kale plants well spaced and in clean cultivation, frequently stirring the soil with a scuffle hoe or rake. Never cultivate deeper than ½ inch, as this damages roots. As plants develop, side-dress with 2 ounces per yard of nitrate of soda or a lighter application of ammonium nitrate. Never allow the plants to stop growing for lack of water;

irrigate from below in early morning. Watch for typical cabbage crop pests—aphids, cabbage loopers, harlequin plant bugs, and the like, and control as recommended under cabbage.

Harvesting is critical. The most edible portion of the plant is the young foliage, just behind the growing point. Of course, the entire terminal rosette is succulent and tender, but to remove it destroys the plant. Gather single leaves into a bucket of ice water, search carefully for insect pests, and cook lightly as quickly as possible.

Cultivars

Scotch or Curled Types

Dwarf Blue Curled Scotch, 50 days; a dwarf, compact selection, leaves very fringed and curled, blue-green.

Dwarf Green Curled Scotch, 55 days; as above, but with white ribs and yellow-green curled blades. Youngest foliage may be used as lettuce.

Evergreen Gem, 50 days; an extremely lacy, bluish strain curled almost as parsley. A particularly good strain, especially in the South.

Tall Scotch, 60 days; seldom grown nowadays, but a taller, somewhat coarser version of the **Dwarf Blue Curled Scotch**.

Vates, 55 days; an especially delicious and tender strain, bluish, curled, from the Virginia Truck Experiment Station. Exceptionally nutritious with a very high vitamin content.

Siberian Types

Blue Siberian (also known as **Sprouts**), 65 days; plant is tall, hardy, and very wide; leaves are coarse with cut and frilled edges.

Early Curled Siberian, 55 days; much like the above but somewhat shorter, mid-green in color, and maturing earlier.

Kohlrabi

Brassica caulorapa   Cabbage Family

This unfamiliar member of the cabbage group is an ideal vegetable for a small home garden; it takes up little space, matures rapidly, allowing follow-up crops, and it is delicious. From the strong root, just above ground the stem swells into a fleshy globe, almost turnip-like in form, and leaves break out from the sides and top of this bulbous stem which is the edible portion. To prepare kohlrabi, bring in the plants, remove the roots and leaves, pare away the thin rind, and slice or dice the fleshy globe; steamed, sauteed, creamed, buttered—it is delicious any way you fix it! Be sure to gather plants early, before any woody inner tissue forms. This is a cold-weather crop; ideal for early spring and fall. It does not stand through summer heat.

Soil Preparation

Soil prepared as for cabbage suits kohlrabi; spade in a deep layer of old manure or enriched compost, top-dress with 3 ounces of 5–10–5 fertilizer per square yard, and fork in. Walk down the planting area to firm the soil.

Planting

You may set plants or directly sow seed. Start plants in flats of any suitable germinating compost; mark off drills ½ inch deep, then sow seeds sparsely and cover. Seed is sown 8 to 10 weeks before the frost-free date; keep warm to germinate, then grow on at 55° to 60° F. in bright light. Transplant to rows on 15- to 18-inch centers, plants 6 inches apart, a week or two before the frost-free date. Firm plants in well; when established, dribble 5–10–5 fertilizer, 2 ounces per yard, along both sides of the row in a 4-inch-wide band 3 inches from the plants. Scratch in the fertilizer.

To grow by direct sowing, three or four weeks before the frost-free date, open shallow drills (½ inch deep), soak the bottom of the drill with hot water if soil is not damp, and sow seeds two or three per inch. Cover, and pat down soil with the back of the rake. When seedlings have three or four true leaves, thin to space plants 6 inches apart. You may lift and transplant surplus seedlings if desired.

Cultivation and Management

As other cabbage relatives, kohlrabi resents deep cultivation; use a scuffle hoe weekly to maintain a shallow dust mulch. Uninterrupted, fast growth produces the most succulent vegetable; if moisture is lacking, water plants generously. Make one or two sowings in spring (more in the North) and again in late summer for a fall crop.

Pests and Diseases

The same insects and diseases that attack cabbage may attack kohlrabi, but because the crop grows mostly in a cold season and is very quick to mature, pests and diseases are almost never a problem.

Cultivars (Cultivar Names May Be Prefixed by "Early")
Prague Special, 44 days; an extremely tender, early sort with large, whitish-green bulbs and few leaves.
Purple Vienna, 55 days; leaves and rind of the bulb the color of red cabbage, bulb white inside; more leaves than *Prague Special.*
White Vienna, 55 days; similar to the above cultivar, but bulb greenish-white and leaves green; leafy.

Leek

Allium porrum   Lily Family

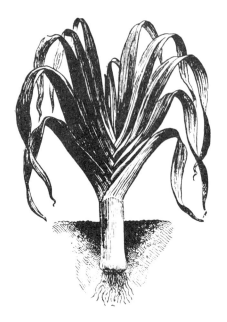

Leeks are among the oldest cultivated vegetables; the ancient Egyptians grew them. They are not at all difficult but are very slow-growing. They are extremely hardy, tolerating more cold than most other vegetables; where winters are not terribly severe, mulch the leeks in late fall and dig them through winter as needed. Leeks are essential for that queen of soups, vichyssoise, and are used in many other gourmet dishes as well as being served as a vegetable.

Soil Preparation

Like all root crops, leeks require very deeply dug soil. Spade in 20 pounds of decayed barnyard manure per square yard in the fall, fork up the ground in earliest spring. Deep, rich, very well-drained loam is best for leeks. They do poorly on very sandy or heavy, tight clay soils.

Planting

You can start leeks in one or two ways, and plant them in one of two ways. For a very long growing season or for an early crop, start seedlings in a flat in late February or early March. Use any good germinating compost, mark off rows in two directions at 1-inch intervals, and sow one or two seeds at each intersection. Cover seeds with ¼ inch germinating compost. A cool room temperature will insure good germination. *Note:* Only fresh seed is viable. Grow seedlings in very bright light, at a night temperature of 40° to 50° F., day temperatures somewhat warmer. Harden off seedlings in the flat when danger of frost is past, cut back tops to one-half or more if very weak, and move to the open garden. The second method is to open a shallow drill—rows 9 to 18 inches apart—and sow seeds two per inch, covering to a depth of ¼ inch. If soil is not moist, carefully soak the bottom of the drill before sowing seed.

Plant leeks on the level (not in trenches), 9 inches apart, rows 9 to 18 inches apart, or in trenches up to 12 inches deep, and 18 to 24 inches apart. Level planting is advisable where soil drains slowly and is not of the best texture; it will be necessary to "hill up" leeks later. Trench-planted leeks, where soil is loamy and fast-draining, can be blanched by soil fill to give nearly a 12-inch white leek.

Cultivation and Management

Hoe leeks and apply liquid manure or liquid fertilizer solution frequently. Water sufficiently often so soil never dries out. Top-dress once or twice with 5–10–5 fertilizer, 2 ounces per running yard on each side of the row a few inches from the plants, or better, with 1 ounce of steamed bonemeal or 1 ounce of superphosphate plus ½ ounce sulfate of potash per running yard.

As plants grow, gradually pull soil in toward the trench-grown leeks (this is the best way) or gradually hill up (broadly) the flat-grown leeks. Keep the plants going right through summer and fall in clean cultivation with sufficient irrigation. Mound with deep straw when the soil is quite cold, or, where deep freezes occur, lift the leeks and store in barely damp sand in a cold, frost-proof place.

Cultivars

Conqueror, 85 days; blue-green foliage, winter hardy, moderately long base.

Elephant, 85 days; early sort, very thick with medium-length stalks.

Giant Musselburgh, 90 days; the standard sort, 2½ to 3 inches thick, medium-long.

Odin, 90 days; gray-green leaves, thick, tender stalks; hardy.

Titan, 70 days; the earliest leek, not hardy, green leaves, 6-inch stalks. Summer use.

Unique, 100 days; blue-green leaves, thick, 7- to 8-inch stalks; delicious, hardy.

Lettuce

Lactuca sativa   Composite Family

Perhaps the oldest of the salad crops (known to be in cultivation in 500 B.C.), lettuce remains a greatly favored salad vegetable today. All lettuces are cool-weather plants; when the temperature exceeds the moderate range lettuce becomes bitter and often plants "bolt," that is, they produce a tall stem with flowers, then seeds, at the top. Some lettuces tolerate light frost. The seasons for lettuce, then, are early spring and fall. If you have a greenhouse or hotbed or cold frame facilities, or even fluorescent lights in a chilly basement, start lettuce seedlings in individual pots some six to eight weeks prior to the last killing frost date for your area, and then set out the young plants a week or ten days before the last killing frost date. If bitter weather should come along you can make paper "hats" from sheets of newspaper to protect the seedlings. By all means grow plenty of fall lettuce, if well grown and covered with boxes or plastic over bitter nights, you can have garden lettuce into very late fall.

The several hundred strains of commercial lettuces fall into four general categories: the crisp head or iceberg types much favored by western truck gardeners and supermarket buyers; the butterhead types sometimes referred to as Boston lettuces (these account for the delicious salads of Europe); the Romaine or cos lettuces grown for people in France and the United States (and for chickens in England and Canada); and leaf lettuce which grows around the world in cool climates, but is particularly favored in the marginal zone between cool and warm in the United States. The first three lettuces need to be grown as individual plants—beginners too often lose their crop of these by allowing crowding, typical of our way of growing leaf lettuces. Leaf lettuces can be grown fairly thickly in the row, but begin to thin them when leaves are about 3 inches tall (big enough for tender salads) so plants are spaced several inches apart by the time the leaves are 6 inches tall.

Lettuce makes a good catch crop. That is, it can be inter-planted between plants of a slow-maturing crop (cabbage, for example) where it will be used up before the slower crop needs the space, or it can be set in between rows of a crop that is just finishing up (late summer beans, for example) to get a start while the main crop is on its way out. In small gardens, lettuces make handsome edging plants. I have seen lettuce growing in window boxes and I know from experience that it matures nicely in a pot so long as the weather remains quite cool. The point is, you can tuck in lettuce almost anywhere because it comes along so quickly. When starting children on gardening I always have them plant leaf lettuce because they will be eating bread, butter and lettuce sandwiches before their attention span wanes. Once I worked out a mosaic bed just with lettuces: yellow-green and ruby leaf lettuces, dark, grass-green, summer Bibb, and the paler green Parris Island Cos. It was a shame to cut any for the table because it made holes in my beautiful design. But we ate all of it!

Soil Preparation

Lettuce will grow on most garden soils if sufficient amounts of fertilizer and some organic matter has been worked in. Commercially, many of the crisp iceberg types are grown on heavy muckland, but these are special; spring lettuces seem to make the finest plants on sandy loam, and fall lettuces do better on silt or even clay loams, probably because they are cooler. Soil for lettuce should have been limed within the past few years, unless it is overlying limestone rock.

If you have grown a heavily manured crop—potatoes, tomatoes, leeks, celery—in your garden last year, that is the place for this spring's lettuce. If you can prepare lettuce soil in the fall, spade in 20 pounds per square yard of barnyard manure or compost. For "spring only" preparation, as early as possible turn in a 2-inch-deep layer of finished compost or very well-decayed barnyard manure. In spring, *after* the soil is worked down for setting in lettuce plants or for sewing seed, top-dress with about 5 ounces of 5–10–10 fertilizer per square yard. When this is down, steel rake or lightly rotary-till the soil to incorporate it.

To plant lettuce for fall use, select an area that was manured for the present season or dress an area with compost or well-rotted manure and spade it in deeply. Mulch with 6 inches of loose straw to cool the soil, and a week or ten days later remove the straw and work down the soil to a seedbed, applying 5–10–10 fertilizer as recommended above. Sow seed or set plants and replace straw to keep soil cool, but as soon as the nights cool down, remove the mulch and go to clean cultivation.

Planting

Most gardeners directly sow lettuce. There are two methods. Draw open a drill with a Warren hoe or the corner of a standard hoe. Rows for head lettuces should be 12 to 18 inches

101

apart; for leaf lettuces 12 to 15 inches apart. The drill for direct sowing should be shallow, not more than 1 inch deep, shallower where soil is heavy. Sow seed sparsely, two to three per inch, and cover with ¼ inch of soil. If the garden soil is not reasonably damp, carefully fill the drill with water and sow seed on the mud. Do not sprinkle the soil-covered row. Seedlings will appear in three to seven days. A broad row for leaf lettuce only is favored in some parts of the country. Mark off rows on 15-inch centers. With a standard hoe, the blade sliding almost parallel to the soil surface, scoop out a blade-width depression about ½ inch deep, depositing the soil on both sides of the broad, shallow, flat-bottomed trench. Scatter in leaf lettuce seeds, two or three per square inch, and rake in soil to cover ¼ inch deep. Pat with the back of the rake to gently compact.

To set lettuce seedlings grown in peat blocks, in individual pots, or lifted from once-transplanted flats, mark off rows spaced as described above and set leaf lettuce plants 9 inches apart in the row; head lettuces 12 inches apart. Set in plants only in late afternoon and water immediately; lettuce seedlings collapse easily.

Where space is minimal and lettuce is a favorite crop, mark off rows of plants to be set later—for tomatoes, eggplant, or peppers—and sow or set lettuces as described above. When it is time to set the other crop, mark off spacings for the plants, remove lettuces where necessary, and set in the summer crop. The new crop can be coming on as the lettuce is used up. Another space-saving method in spring or fall is to mark off rows for cabbages, brussels sprouts, broccoli, or another wide species; set these in, then rake down the space in each row between the plants and open drills for lettuce seed or set in a few lettuce plants. The lettuce will mature before the other crop spreads too widely.

Cultivation and Management

Keep lettuce in clean cultivation. The use of mulch of any sort invites snails and slugs which will be plentiful enough, even with clean cultivation. Avoid deep hoeing close to the plants as they collapse if roots are disturbed on a bright day. After seedlings (either from directly sown seed or those that have been set in) have grown of two to three weeks, dribble nitrate of soda along both sides of the row, a band 4 inches wide and 4 inches from the bases of the plants, 2 ounces per running yard, and rake this in shallowly. To thin leaf lettuce, wait until late afternoon; water the crop and an hour or so later, as the sun goes down, thin the plants. If you pull seedlings in the morning and a breeze comes up during the sunny midday, the entire planting may collapse and wilt due to soil disturbance!

Pests and Diseases

Few insects bother lettuce, though occasionally aphids move in. These can be discouraged with a light malathion spray or dust. Use pellets (kept off the plants) for slug and snail control. Several diseases harass lettuce: damping-off, which destroys germinating seedlings; bottom rot; sclerotinia drop; and gray mold—all of which affect leaves. If your garden tends to be damp, plant lettuce on shallow ridges and space plants far apart. Remove and destroy sick plants, thinned plants, and finished plants from the garden. Avoid planting lettuce where it grew a year previously. Usually these steps provide clean plants. If leaf diseases persist, use a vegetable garden fungicide dust.

Cultivars

Crisp Head (Iceberg)
Great Lakes 6238, 94 days; medium-green, recommended for late sowing.
Ithaca, 85 days; medium-green.
Pennlake, 88 days; dark-green, good early cropper.
Premier Great Lakes, 93 days; start indoors early for early maturing crop.
Stokes Evergreen, 95 days; quite cold-resistant.

Butterhead
Bibb, 58 days; old-time favorite; bolts with first summer heat.
Buttercrunch, 64 days; rather upright, slowest to bolt with heat. Delicious.
Butter King, 64 days; very large, reasonably slow to bolt. Good.
Dark Green Boston, 68 days; medium-sized, very tender; no good in heat.
Summer Bibb, 62 days; all the good qualities of **Bibb** but more heat-tolerant.
White Boston, 66 days; outstanding European strain, does not tolerate heat.

Loose-Leaf

Black-Seeded Simpson, 45 days; old favorite, still among the best. Lime-green.

Grand Rapids, 45 days; light-green, old, reliable sort. Commercial strains available.

Oak Leaf, 45 days; delicate texture and flavor, handsome leaves.

Ruby, 45 days; the tenderest sort, leaves dark red, delicious if used when young.

Salad Bowl, 48 days; the best-tasting and easiest to grow of the new strains.

Slobolt, 48 days; A very high-quality lettuce, tolerates some heat. Good for outdoor growing and in the forcing frame.

Romaine or Cos

Parris Island Cos, 76 days; 10 inches high, tight cylindrical heads. Choice.

Valamine Cos, 75 days; similar to **Parris Island** but resists mildew as well as mosaic.

Malabar Spinach

Basella rubra (B. alba in Hort.) Madeira-Vine Family

Of relatively recent introduction, this succulent climber
thrives in hot weather. Those who tout it claim vast nutritional
benefits. It is easy to grow, but the flavor leaves quite a lot to be
desired and the texture is best described as slimy.

Soil Preparation

Spread a generous layer of old barnyard manure or
enriched compost along a sunny fence and fork it in deeply. Top-
dress the soil with 5–10–5 fertilizer, 4 ounces per square yard,
and rake down the loose soil.

Planting

When soil is thoroughly warm, open a shallow drill about
1 inch deep, soak the soil at the bottom (use hot water if soil is
not quite warm), and scatter seeds in sparsely. Cover with ½
inch of pulverized soil and pat down with the back of the rake.

Cultivation and Management

As seedlings appear, thin to stand 6 inches or more apart.
Water seedlings at biweekly intervals with a liquid fertilizer solution to encourage rapid growth. When a foot high, cut back to 6
inches (use these leafy tips for salad or for cookery); this
encourages branching. Train the shoots up the fence and harvest
tips and young leaves frequently.

There are no cultivars of Malabar spinach. Incidentally,
the name is a misnomer. Botanically this is familiarly identified
as Malabar nightshade. Small wonder that seedmen changed that
epithet!

Melons

Muskmelon

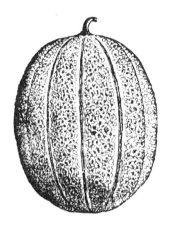

Cucumis melo   Cucumber Family

The melons with a central cavity (as contrasted with the solid-fleshed watermelons) are of very ancient culture. Several botanical varieties are recognized, as follows:

C. melo var. *cantalupensis*, Cantaloupe: a European melon with a hard rind, rough but not netted. Very superior fruit; not grown in the U.S., though the name is used here.

var. *chito*, Mango Melon: orange, shading to purplish, white-fleshed, cucumber-like flesh used for preserves and pickles.

var. *dudaim*, Pomegranate Melon: small, inedible fruits grown for their intense fragrance (as pomanders).

var. *flexuosus*, Snake Melon: long, slender, twisted melons with inedible flesh; a curiosity.

var. *inodorus*, Winter Melon: fruits with either smooth, corrugated, or scaly rind, unscented, flesh white, light green or orange, delicious; these ripen late and store reasonably well, including the difficult **Honey Dew**, **Casaba**, **Crenshaw**, and **Persian** melons.

var. *reticulatus*, Muskmelon: with soft to leathery rind always at least partially netted, musky scented, flesh varying from yellowish- to reddish-orange to pale green. These are the common American muskmelons and "cantaloupes."

Soil Preparation

Like other members of this family, the muskmelons and their relatives are gross feeders, thriving best in a sandy loam generously enriched with old barnyard manure or compost and complete fertilizer that is slightly on the acid side (pH 6.2 to 6.8). In the open garden, mark out hills on 4-foot centers on soil that has been worked up as follows: top-dress fall-spaded soil in mid-spring with up to 1 bushel of decayed manure or old compost and 5 ounces of 5–10–10 fertilizer (if this is unavailable, use 5–10–5 plus ½ ounce agricultural potash) per square yard, and fork deeply to incorporate the manure and fertilizer uniformly throughout the soil. On very light soil, increase the manure application. On heavy loam, such as clay loam, after the bed is prepared, at each planting site mound a few shovels of compost or manure, lightly forking it through the soil, and rake more soil over it to achieve a raised hill on which to plant.

Planting

When night air temperature is constant, above 60° F., plant seeds of muskmelons on each hill, three or four seeds per station, and cover with ½ inch of soil; tamp lightly to compact the soil around the seeds. If soil is on the dry side, rake out a shallow planting saucer, fill with water two or three times, sow seeds, cover with dry soil, and tamp gently. Where seasons are short, fill small flowerpots or old wooden strawberry boxes with seed germinating mix or with prepared garden loam and start seeds indoors as much as eight weeks prior to your estimated setting-out time. When transplanting, disturb the roots as little as possible.

Cultivation and Management

Keep melon plants in clean cultivation; as roots are shallow, frequent work with a scuffle hoe is best, but a conventional hoe held at a shallow angle does the job—so does a garden rake pulled through the soil every day or two to dislodge fresh seedlings. In humid areas, keep melons in clean cultivation the whole season. Where mildew is not a serious problem, when seedlings begin to sprawl apply a light, loose mulch of fresh straw to a depth of 4 to 5 inches. At about this time (plants will have 4 to 5 leaves) dress a broad band around each hill with 4 ounces of nitrate of soda or 2 ounces of ammonium nitrate. Alternatively, apply dark tea-colored manure water to each hill at two-week intervals.

Water is critical; when melon vines wilt, they are in trouble. Irrigate frequently, preferably by letting a hose seep at each hill (or *see* Cucumber, page 84, for the sunken tin can method).

Pests and Diseases

The same pests and diseases that attack cucumbers affect melons; *see* Cucumber, page 84, for control of diseases, and insect pests.

Cultivars

Dozens of quite good muskmelon cultivars are available to us; especially recommended for home use are the newer sorts with vines of limited length, making them more suitable for the small garden.

Burpee Hybrid, 70 days; oval melons, heavily netted and ribbed, deep orange flesh, small cavity; average 4½ pounds. Excellent.

Delicious 51, 82 days; oval, netted, shallow-ribbed rind, sweet, delicious dark-orange flesh; to 5 pounds. Does not ship well but excellent for home use.

Harper Hybrid, 80 days; an F_1 hybrid, nearly round, netted but unribbed fruit, flesh thick; fragrant, juicy, and sweet, one of the best; melons to 5½ pounds; fusarium wilt-tolerant.

Luscious, 78 days; long oval, netted, shallowly ribbed fruits with deep orange, very high-quality flesh; melons to 4½ pounds; fusarium wilt-resistant, mildew-tolerant.

Sampson, 80 days; F_1 hybrid with oval fruit, heavily netted and scarcely ribbed, flesh deep orange, sweet; melons to 5 pounds; tolerant of powdery mildew and fusarium wilt.

Saticoy, 85 days; F_1 hybrid, fruits oval, coarsely netted and slightly ribbed; fruit deep orange, thick, very sweet and solid; melons to 4 pounds; resistant to fusarium wilt and powdery mildew.

Short 'n' Sweet, 78 days; melons with irregularly netted rind; round, very sweet, deep flesh; fruit to 4 pounds; tolerant of mildew. This melon grows almost in bush form, making it very valuable for small gardens.

Winter Melons

Generally speaking, the winter melons are beyond the average home gardener as they produce under only very specialized soil and climate conditions. But growers south of Zone 4 may wish to try these:

Honey Dew Green, 115 days; nearly round, with thick, white rind and fairly thick, almost white, juicy sweet flesh; melons creamy yellow at maturity, about 5½ pounds; not disease-resistant.

Tam-dew, 90 days; a broad, oval melon with smooth, hard rind and thick, very juicy and sweet green flesh, small seed cavity; matures at 5½ to 6½ pounds; not disease-resistant but somewhat tolerant.

Watermelon

Citrullus vulgaris   Cucumber Family

Watermelons were grown in America in the early 1600's and soon became a favorite crop of the native Indians. Because the vines of most sorts run fifteen feet or more, these are not recommended for the average home garden. However, in recent years a few varieties with quite small but tasty fruits and shorter vines have become available. They still are space-consuming. One way to save space is to grow your watermelons on the old compost heap.

Soil Preparation

As for muskmelon; lay out hills on an 8 by 8 foot grid and allow at least 8 feet beyond the last hill for an adjacent row of another vegetable crop.

Planting

As for muskmelon; usually plants are thinned to not more than three per hill.

Cultivation and Management

As for muskmelon. Because watermelons take several months to produce the vines, they have to be kept healthy from the beginning. Start to dust or spray for insect and disease control when vines are small and continue until nearly harvest time. By all means, keep watermelons in clean cultivation, either on the soil or on a deep straw mulch.

Pests and Diseases

See Muskmelon, page 106; Cucumber, page 83.

Cultivars

Black Diamond, 88 days; very high quality, an older sort making stubby oval, very dark-green melons to 125 pounds;

choice but rampant.

Charleston Gray, 85 days; a long, pale watermelon with extremely dark-red flesh of high quality, rampant, and not disease-resistant, but remains a market favorite.

Crimson Sweet, 90 days; from the research program at Kansas State University, a disease-tolerant cultivar producing dark-green, nearly round melons in the 20-pound range, top-quality flesh.

Dixie Queen, 80 days; 40-pound, dark-green, nearly round melons; very sugary flesh, extremely vigorous vines; some strains are disease-tolerant.

Seedless Hybrid 313, 90 days; unfortunately, this is sold under several names, but is the only top-quality, sugary sweet, seedless melon on the market today; melons are round, to 15 pounds, striped dark and light green, flesh bright red, crisp. This has to be planted (for pollination) with a few vines of another sort.

Stokes' Sugar Hybrid, 70 days; an oblong, medium-green melon averaging 15 pounds, dark rose-red flesh, sugary; a heavy yielder; and disease-resistant.

Sugar Baby, 73 days; rather dark green, round melons to 8 pounds with usually high-quality crisp medium-red flesh. Not the very best, but fits the home garden (and refrigerator) handily.

Yellow Baby, 75 days; from Taiwan, a very superior stubby-oblong melon, striped, to 10 pounds, with very thin rind, few seeds, and brilliant yellow flesh which is better tasting than most red sorts; not especially disease-tolerant but usually makes an early crop.

Citron Types

Green Seeded, 98 days; similar to the above sort, but fruits slightly larger, and flesh dark green with no staining; most commonly encountered as "candied citron" for culinary use.

Red Seeded, 95 days; round, 10- to 12-pound melons, striped; very prolific; produces meaty melons (not good "as is") especially suited for preserving.

Mustard

Brassica juncea   Mustard Family

Mustard greens are favored provender in Southern states. Northern gardeners find the harsh texture and biting tang not to their taste in most cases. Still, the plants grow easily and on most soils and are very high in vitamins. The selected cultivars listed below are all cold-weather crops, bolting to bloom with the onset of warm weather. In the South, grow as a winter vegetable, in the North, plant in very early spring or in late summer for a fall crop.

Soil Preparation

Sandy loam or loam gives the best plants, but any well-turned, humus-enriched, and fertilized soil will produce a quick crop of mustard greens. Just before sowing, broadcast 3 pounds of 5–10–5 fertilizer per 100 square feet and rake it into the top 2 or 3 inches. Sow seed immediately.

Planting

Sow-broadcast or, better, mark off rows on 10-inch centers and open ½-inch-deep drills. Sow 1 to 2 seeds per inch and cover with ½ inch of pulverized soil. Pat down firmly with the back of the steel rake. Seedlings appear in 5 to 10 days depending on strain, soil temperature, and soil moisture.

Cultivation and Management

Mustard is a quick crop. Do not thin the seedlings. Keep the soil loose with frequent use of a scuffle hoe or other hoe; water when rainfall is less than ½ inch per week.

Few pests bother mustard; flea beetles may show up; apply malathion or diazinon. Harvest as soon as leaves are eating size; they go tough, stringy, and bitter quickly.

Cultivars

Florida Broad Leaf, 40 days; vigorous, upright, leaves thick and smooth.

Fordhook Fancy, 40 days; curled, fringed, dark-green leaves; mild.

Giant Southern Curled, 45 days; very large, upright, leaves crumpled and curled.

Green Wave, 45 days; small, dense plants with frilled leaves; tender and mild.

Ostrich Plume, 35 days; large plants; curliest, most frilled leaves of all.

Tendergreen, 30 days; slow to bolt in heat, cold-resistant. One of the best.

Okra

Hibiscus esculentus   Mallow Family

Okra, or gumbo, is a hot-weather crop. Wait until soil is warm and days and nights are summery before sowing seed. In cool climates gardeners sometimes open planting drills and warm the soil with repeated waterings of scalding water prior to sowing seed. Okra grows best on deeply prepared, fertile soil that is never dried deeply. The plants do not do well on poor, shallow, or heavy soil. Five to ten plants per member of the family provide ample okra pods for eating as a vegetable, for soups, and for freezing.

Soil Preparation

In the autumn, dress the bed area with manure, 20 pounds per square yard, and spade deeply. Double-digging is advisable in all but the most loamy soils. If you must prepare the okra bed in spring, do it as early as possible, spading in manures and composts. Let the soil fallow until hot weather or use it for spring crops such as radishes, lettuce, or peas. Just before okra planting time, dress the soil with 6 ounces per square yard of 5–10–5 fertilizer and fork in thoroughly.

Planting

Mark out rows on 3-foot centers. Open drills not more than 1½ inches deep; if soil is not moist, flood the drill with hot water; take care not to dislodge the soil. Sow okra seeds at 2-inch intervals (or closer); thin 6-inch-high seedlings to stand 12 to 18 inches apart.

Cultivation and Management

Keep okra in clean cultivation; irrigate freely during dry periods. Apply a side-dressing of 5–10–5 fertilizer in a band 4 inches wide, 4 inches from the bases of the plants, 2 ounces per running yard, on both sides of the rows. Rake it in. Pick okra pods when quite young for best eating. The ribbed strains, particularly, get woody rather quickly.

Cultivars

Clemson Spineless, 56 days; slightly ribbed pods of excellent quality. Good color.

Emerald, 60 days; pods dark green, smooth, tender. Developed by Campbell Soup Company.

Perkins Mammoth Long Pod, 50 days; dark green, tapered, ribbed pods. A commercial strain.

Red Okra, 60 days; a new novelty sort; red pods turn green when cooked.

Spineless Green Velvet, 58 days; pods mid-green, smooth, round, prolific.

Onion

Allium cepa   Lily Family

Onions are an ancient vegetable; today we use them while small and tender as a salad vegetable, when somewhat larger for eating cooked or for pickling, when full-sized for baking or for slicing, and as a seasoning for many other dishes. In your garden I recommend you begin with onion plants or sets because onions from seed are tedious (instructions are given for the ambitious, however). Try to space your plantings so you may harvest for the various uses. In general, table onions fall into two classes: the American types, which are pungent (including cultivars such as **Early Yellow Globe, Ebenezer, Yellow Globe Danvers,** all yellow sorts, **Southport White Globe,** a good white, and **Red Wethersfield** and **Southport Red Globe** as reds); and the foreign, sweet sorts which include the various Bermuda and Spanish types. For home use, the newer hybrid sorts cannot be recommended too highly as these are of finest table quality, most keep quite well, and they grow vigorously.

Soil Preparation

Onions will grow on most soils so long as drainage is good and the soil has been very thoroughly worked, but loams and muck soils give best and easiest results. Onions respond to ample organic matter in the soil and require high amounts of nutrients. Plant onions where a heavily manured crop grew last year, or spade in and till thoroughly 3 to 4 bushel basketfuls of well-rotted manure or compost per 100 square feet. Top-dress with 5–10–5 fertilizer, 3½ pounds per 100 square feet, and fork this in. Onion soil needs more forking and raking than most garden soil.

Planting

Onions may be raised from seed, from plants, or from dried sets. To grow plants or sets, in early spring (onions tolerate the last two or three frosts) mark off rows on 12- to 15-inch centers and open trenches with a Warren hoe or standard hoe. The trench should be about 2 inches deep. Set plants or sets 3 inches apart in the row; cover plants so just the tips show. Sets should be covered with 1 to 3 inches of soil depending on use and variety as well as heaviness of soil. Heavier soils require shallower planting.

Cultivation and Management

Always keep onions in clean cultivation, with loose soil. Hand-weed frequently and use a hand scratcher to loosen the soil between plants. The best tool for cultivating between rows is the scuffle hoe, but any tool that gives a shallow dust mulch will work well. When plants begin to grow, apply a trickle of ammonium nitrate or nitrate of soda down both sides of each row 3 to 4 inches from the plants. Onions should not be allowed to go bone-dry; water deeply at weekly intervals through drought periods. When the below-ground portion of the onions are finger-sized, pull every other one for scallions. When the bulbs are walnut-sized, again, pull every other one, but for creaming, boiling, or pickling. Allow the remainder to mature. When tops break over, lift the plants with a fork and lay then on top of the row to cure for three or four days (in extremely hot climates remove them to an airy, shady place), then spread or hang them in the garage for a week or two to become quite dry outside. Sack in mesh bags or tie in bunches and store in a cool, dry, well-ventilated place. Humidity is the bane of stored onions. Frost will destroy them.

Pests and Diseases

Onion maggot, a larvae of a small fly, may bore into the onions, damaging the interior, and onion thrips, a nearly microscopic leaf-sucking insect, attacks the foliage. For maggots, apply diazinon at weekly intervals beginning in early spring; for thrips, spray with methoxychlor frequently. Few diseases trouble onions if the soil is clean; Bordeaux spray or zineb will reduce foliage diseases. If your onions fail to keep because of fungus problems (molds, black or pink), plant only resistant varieties.

Special Instructions for Onions

To grow onions from seed, start fresh (only) seed in flats; use any suitable germinating medium, sow seed ¼ inch deep in close drills. Or plant directly in properly spaced rows in the garden; sow seed two or three per inch, in ½-inch-deep drills, and cover with ¼ inch pulverized soil, or, better, with milled sphagnum or pulverized compost. Pull in soil to bed level when seedlings are 2 inches high. Transplant flatted seedlings when of manageable size and when danger of frost is past. These make better onions if set in a deep trench as described for onion plants or sets.

Some people prefer to grow just "green" onions. For

these, plant plants or sets of **Beltsville Bunching, Japanese Bunching, Egyptian (Hardy Top** or **Tree** onion), or **Multiplier** strains. These are non-bulb forming. The perennial ones never set seed; set them at the garden edge and leave them alone, pulling as needed. Always take some of the bulblets from the tall seed stems and plant them to keep the stock going.

Cultivars

(Maturity Dates from Seed; Sets and Plants Take About Half as Long)

Aristocrat, 105 days; a yellow American hybrid sort with some disease tolerance.

Canada Maple, 98 days; an early American hybrid; disease-resistant and stores well.

Chieftain, 115 days; a select hybrid Spanish sort; copper-colored, mild, stores well.

Early Yellow Globe, 100 days; an old standby; stores only moderately well.

Fiesta, 110 days; a very select Spanish type, sweet hybrid; stores well. Seeds must be started in mid-winter in flats to go to the garden in mid-spring.

Golden Mosque, 105 days; one of the better "set" types; makes a round, bright yellow onion when mature (sets are spindle-shaped); keeps well.

Hickory, 99 days; a very hard, American-type onion that keeps well. For the North.

Northern Oak, 108 days; a large, hard storage onion of gold-brown color; pungent.

Riverside Sweet Spanish, 115 days; a very mild, delicate onion, to 6 inches, delicious; does not store well.

Southport Red Globe, 100 days; strong flavor, red skin, white inside, keeps well.

Southport White Globe, 65 days; a good onion for pulling for bunching, not for storing.

Stuttgarter, 120 days; this is the standard yellow set of garden shops and supermarkets. It is a good onion for light soil, keeps well if cured properly.

White Ebenezer, 100 days; a pungent onion of merit, only for table use.

White Portugal, 100 days; a mild onion forming a globe while small, ideal for pickling.

Yellow Ebenezer, 100 days; a very fine yellow onion, somewhat pungent but not "strong," keeps well if cured properly.

Yellow Globe, 98 days; a moderate-sized, rather pungent, round onion that keeps well for winter cooking.

Parsley

Petroselinum crispum   Carrot Family

Parsley is a handy thing to have in every garden; technically it seems to belong with the "herbs" as it is not used as a vegetable in itself (except for the **Hamburg** strain), but since it has been bred and developed into cultivars as no other herbs have been, let's call it a vegetable. It is a cold-weather biennial; like many of the carrot family, seed is slow to germinate, and many lie for as long as six weeks. Cool soil and cool weather favor development of strong seedlings. Parsley plants grow in the leafy stage through the first summer, fall, and winter; the following spring a few new leaves and a flower-spike are produced; if seed sets, the plant dies. You can prolong the life of parsley plants by pinching out bloom shoots as they appear, but it is easier and the plants are of better quality if you keep a new crop coming on annually, discarding the old as the new plants begin to produce.

Soil Preparation

Parsley thrives in a deep, rich loam. Very light or very heavy soils have to be amended with great quantities of compost or manure to be suitable. Prior to sowing seed, dress the soil with 4 ounces of 5–10–5 fertilizer per square yard, and work it through the top 3 or 4 inches with a steel rake. Organic gardeners use 2 ounces each of bonemeal and hoof meal, and 1 ounce of potash per square yard.

Planting

Sow parsley seeds two or three weeks before the frost-free date, even earlier where springs are long and drawn out. Mark off rows at the edge of the garden as the crop stands for 12 months or longer. Usually one row is ample, for multiple rows, use a 12-inch spacing. Rake down the soil, open a ½-inch-deep drill, and sow two to three seeds per inch; scatter in one or two radish seeds per inch to mark the row. Cover seeds with ¼ to ½-inch of pulverized soil and tamp down with the back of the rake. Remember that parsley often is very slow to germinate.

Cultivation and Management

Hand-weed the row and with a small hand tool cultivate

in close to the seedlings; for several weeks they are weak. When they develop their thickened roots they will take rougher treatment. When plants have several true leaves, dress the row, 2 ounces per running yard, each side, with 5–10–5 fertilizer or with 1 ounce of nitrate of soda or ammonium nitrate (bloodmeal also is very good and discourages rabbits but attracts dogs). The side-dressing should be a 4-inch-wide band, 3 inches from the plants. Keep in clean cultivation. Through summer, if drought occurs, water parsley deeply but not too frequently.

Pests and Diseases

Few pests and diseases bother vigorously growing parsley plants; occasionally yellow, black, and white ringed caterpillars strip leaves from a few plants; you can spray these with malathion or diazinon, hand-pick and destroy them, or, as I do, nurture them because they will make the beautiful black swallowtail butterflies that are as important to a beautiful garden as the parsley garnish is to a beautiful rib roast. The plants will restore the lost leaves in a few weeks.

Cultivars

Banquet, 76 days; wide plants with dark-green, tightly frilled leaves. Winters well.

Bravour, 75 days; similar to the above (another European strain), but slightly taller.

Darki, 77 days; very dark green, tight, crisped and frilled. European gold medal sort.

Deep Green, 70 days; dark-green, coarsely frilled strain; an old standby.

Extra Triple Curled, 75 days; finely cut, dark-green French strain.

Improved Perfection, 80 days; a taller sort, dark green, leaves much frilled; good for frames.

Italian Giant, 90 days; to 3 feet, resembles celery; immense yields of plain leaves.

Paramount, 85 days; to 12 inches, dark green, densely frilled. Fine home garden strain.

Plain Dark Green Italian, 78 days; a celery-leaved sort, leaves flat; for flavor.

The parsleys grown for edible roots (prepare as parsnips) are:

Hamburg Rooted, 90 days; tops and roots both fine-flavored; ideal for soups.

Record, 88 days; large white roots of superior quality. Use leaves, too.

Parsnip

Pastinaca sativa   Carrot Family

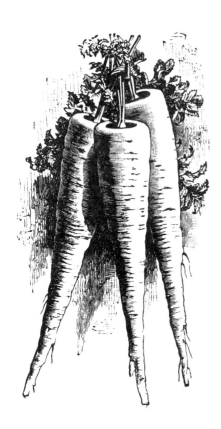

Parsnips are the roots of a biennial plant which we grow as long-season annual. These can be a problem in the small garden as they tie up an entire row for the whole summer. Given proper soil preparation, parsnip roots develop into very large, tender, flavorful vegetables; in poor soil or poorly worked soil, roots are small, crooked, apt to be stringy, and are of only moderate flavor. Where amateur (and professional) gardening competition is stiff, growers go to great extremes to produce perfect parsnips; with a posthole digger they excavate 6- or 8-inch cylinders to 4 feet deep at 15-inch intervals and fill these with carefully sifted mixtures of well-rotted barnyard manure, friable loam, and root fertilizers. Two or three seeds are sown on top of each of these filled spots; seedlings are later thinned to single plants, and plants are coddled with dilute manure water throughout the growing season. The result of all this is a crop of nearly yard-long, perfectly straight, milk-white, perfectly formed and flavored parsnip roots that are the very devil to dig up. You can grow perfectly delicious 10- to 15-inch ones with one-tenth the effort.

Soil Preparation

The best soil is light to medium loam, never heavy clay loam. Deep digging is essential. Even if you only shallowly turn the rest of your garden, double-dig the parsnip row, or at least spade it with a sharpshooter. Plant parsnips along one end of the garden where they will be out of the way, as they go in early and remain until after frost. A row of parsnips through the middle of the garden is a mistake. If your ground has been deeply dug and manured in the fall, in spring dress it with 2 ounces of bonemeal and 1 ounce of sulfate of potash per square yard; contrary to usual procedure, fork this through the top 12 inches or more. Parsnips go in two or three weeks before the last killing frost, so soil preparation must be underway as early as possible.

Planting

Mark out rows of 15- to 18-inch centers and open drills about 1 inch deep. Americans usually sow 3 or 4 seeds per inch, plants to be thinned radically later. In Europe, gardeners sow 3 or 4 seeds at 9- to 12-inch intervals, which certainly is a less wasteful method. Cover seed with pulverized soil to a depth of ½ inch in medium loam, to 1 inch in sandy loam. Never compact the soil. If your soil tends to crust at all, over-sow the parsnip seed with a few radish seeds; the sturdy radish seedlings will break the soil crust and also identify the row. Parsnip seeds germinate in about three weeks at an average temperature of 60° F.

When seedlings have three or four true leaves, water generously at midday and in late afternoon thin to stand at least 4 to 5 inches apart, twice that gives finer-quality roots. Parsnip seedlings are extremely fragile; treat them gently.

Cultivation and Management

Keep parsnips in clean cultivation, or, where summers are extremely warm, mulch during the hottest weather with a deep, porous layer of loose straw. Never allow the soil to dry deeply, but irrigate well away from the plants when watering becomes necessary. Very dilute manure water is the only summer fertilizer; high soil fertility from soluble chemicals causes roots to be covered with hair roots.

Pests and Diseases

Insect pests and diseases of parsnips are the same as those attacking carrots; take the same precautions and use the same treatments.

Cultivars

All-America, 105 days; A moderately short, early thickening sort, small core, fine quality.

Harris' Model, 120 days; the finest American parsnip, medium-long, very smooth, fine-textured tissue of excellent flavor.

Hollow Crown and *Hollow Crown Improved,* 120 days; better form and quality than the All-America; stores well. The "Improved" selections are best.

Peanuts, Groundnuts, Goobers

Arachia hypogaea   Legume Family

Northern gardeners seldom think of peanuts as plants to grow, while many home gardens in the South have their peanut patch. Peanuts will grow wherever a crop of corn can be matured, and with their soaring cost, you might consider planting some. This is a marvelous crop for the children; not only is it fairly foolproof, but throughout the long season the plants do strange things. To sow, you must shell out the peanuts; plants pop up in a few days and soon blossoms, usually yellow, appear. There are two sorts, the sterile, showy ones, and the more important but insignificant-looking small ones which are fertile. After these are fertilized the pod-stalk begins to elongate, growing downward, and soon the burgeoning pod is shoved into the soil where development continues and is completed. Just before frost, with the spading fork, you lift the crop. Properly managed, substantial numbers of peanuts can be grown in a small area. It really pays to have a small patch given over solely to the peanuts as they are an all-summer crop.

Soil Preparation

Peanuts grow best on a light, sandy soil, but will grow on any well-worked soil. The plot must not be recently manured; if the soil is heavy, spade as early in spring (fall is better) as possible, incorporating vast amounts of old, old compost to loosen the clay. A neutral pH is best. At planting time, top-dress the area with 3 ounces per square yard of 2–10–10 fertilizer or just superphosphate and potassium sulfate. Peanuts, being legumes, furnish their own nitrates so long as the soil is kept loose.

Planting

Wait until the soil is thoroughly warm—late May to early June. Rake out the soil, mark off rows on 30-inch centers, and rake into low, broad, row-long mounds. On very sandy soil omit this crowning. Open drills 2 inches deep, and sow seeds four per foot. Later, thin to one or two per foot.

Cultivation and Management

Use your pronged cultivator to keep soil thoroughly loosened throughout the peanut patch. When blossoms form in four to six weeks, take care working near the plants not to break off earthbound pod-stalks. Continue cultivation throughout summer. Peanuts thrive on hot, dry weather. To harvest, just before frost, work one side of each row with a spading fork, inserting and prying. Then return down the other side, inserting, prying, and lifting. Shake the earth from the clusters of peanuts and lay the plants in the sun to air-dry for a few days. Later, hang to cure (unless the weather is hot and dry enough for field curing) and gather the peanuts into mesh bags.

Pests and Diseases

Corn earworms and borers sometimes attack peanut stalks, wireworms and white grubs may attack tender below-ground pods. Fungus and bacterial diseases usually are not a problem unless the soil is heavy and the season long and wet. Regular spraying or dusting with methoxychlor or malathion will control many insect pests, and usually fungicides are not advisable.

Preparation for Use

Raw peanuts are used in certain confections, such as peanut brittle, where they are cooked during candy-making. To roast, put whole peanuts (in shells) in a shallow pan in a 300° F. oven and stir frequently.

Cultivars

Early Spanish, 110 days; bunch-type plant, two or three small, sweet peanuts per pod.

Jumbo Virginia, 120 days; large, sprawling plant, one or two huge peanuts per pod, good quality, but plants almost too large for home growing.

Red Tennessee, 115 days; large plants, large red peanuts, two to five per pod.

Virginia, 115 days; bunch-type, large bush, two to three large nuts per pod.

Garden Peas

Pisum sativum   Legume Family

For centuries peas were allowed to mature and the dried seeds cooked into pease porrige. In the last 150 years peas have come to be used as green vegetables and the number of varieties has increased. Peas are a cold-weather crop; summer heat soon wilts down the vines and pods become harsh, peas flavorless. Plant peas in spring well before the frost-free date, especially in the southern part of the pea range (in the deep South peas are a winter crop). In many parts of the country a late summer planting will produce another good crop during the fall months. While tall pea cultivars are space-demanding, the dwarf sorts may be closely planted and even one or two double rows in a tiny garden will more than pay their way. Always plant wrinkled peas; smooth ones lack sugar.

Soil Preparation

Peas thrive in a light sandy soil but will grow in heavier soils well worked with plenty of coarse, decayed manure or compost. Also, peas are heavy users of fertilizer, especially phosphates and potash. Plant peas where a heavily manured crop grew last year, or in the fall or late winter dress the area with 3 bushels of compost or manure per 100 square feet and spade this in. Just before sowing seed, dress the pea area with 2–10–10 fertilizer, 1 pound per 100 square feet, and rake it into the top 3 or 4 inches. Organic gardeners substitute 2 ounces of bonemeal and 1 ounce each of hoof meal and potash per square yard. Pea soil should be nearly neutral.

Planting

To save space, plant peas in double rows. Mark off centers for dwarf varieties at 30-inch intervals, for taller sorts at 40-inch intervals. At each center, open two parallel rows 10 inches apart. The drills should be about 2 inches deep. Scatter peas generously along the row, eight to ten per foot, and cover to a depth of 1 to 1½ inches, depending on lightness of soil. Press down with the back of the rake or walk down the rows. Sow peas very early (they germinate in five to 8 days at a soil temperature of 50° F.) and make successive sowings at two- to three-week intervals, depending on your summer season.

Cultivation and Management

As peas come up, keep the soil stirred between the rows and along the outsides of the rows with a pronged cultivator. Pea roots fix air nitrogen, and well-aerated soil is essential to best growth. If plants are slow, dribble 5–10–5 fertilizer, 2 ounces per yard, along just the outsides of the double rows. Dwarf sorts require no staking as the peas will reach across the space between rows and twine together, supporting themselves. Intermediate and taller sorts require support. An easy way to provide support is to keep a row-long piece of chicken wire or other wire fencing handy. Lay it out, thread pieces of ¼-inch construction iron rod through it every 5 feet, and stand this temporary support between the two rows in each pair. Or cut twiggy branches from treetops and shove a thick row of these, butts downward, in the space between the pea rows. Never let your peas lack for air or water. Cultivate deeply and frequently, and water if rainfall is less than ½ inch per week.

Pick peas as quickly as the pods fill, and pick daily for a continued set of new pods.

Pests and Diseases

Aphids sometimes cover young pea vines; spray with malathion, diazinon, or nicotine sulphate. Various fungi attack the foliage, especially powdery mildew during warm, humid weather. Early cropping is the best defense, using resistant strains is another good defense; spraying or dusting is usually futile. Several root rot fungi may destroy a pea planting before it gets started. Always plant treated seeds—these will be colored, usually pink. For extra-vigorous plants, treat your peas with a garden pea bacterial inoculum which sets off the nitrogen-fixing action in the roots. The inoculum will not be harmed by the fungicide coating on the seeds.

Cultivars

(Only Good-Flavored, Wrinkle-Seeded (Sweet) Sorts Are Listed)

Alderman (Telephone), 74 days; 4–5-foot vines, 5-inch pods, well-filled. Fine quality.

Banquet, 62 days; 1½–2-foot vines, 3-inch pods, small, very tender peas.

Freezonian, 63 days; 2½-foot vines, 3½-inch pods, large, very sweet peas.

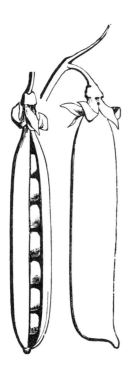

Frosty, 64 days; 2¼-foot vines, 3½-inch pods in pairs, fine quality.

Greater Progress, 62 days; 1½-foot vines, 4-inch pods, large, good-quality peas.

Green Arrow, 68 days; 2-foot vines; 4½-inch pods with small, dark-green, sweet peas. Tolerates mildew and fusarium wilt.

Laxtonian, 62 days; 1½-foot vines, 3½-inch pods with large, sweet peas.

Laxton's Progress, 58 days; 1½-foot vines, 3½-inch pods with very choice, small peas.

Lincoln, 65 days; 2½-foot vines, 3-inch pods, disease-tolerant. One of the best.

Little Marvel, 60 days; 1½-foot vines, 3-inch pods, the sweetest, best, early pea.

Potlach, 75 days; 2-foot vines, 4-inch pods, peas sugary and quite large.

Sparkle, 60 days; 1¼-foot vines, 2½ – 3-inch pods, early and very delicious.

Thomas Laxton, 55 days; 2½ – 3-foot vines, 3½-inch pods, earliest taller sort.

Wando, 65 days; 2½-foot vines, 3-inch pods, stands some heat, good-quality peas.

Black-Eyed Peas,
Southern Table Peas, Cow Peas

Vigna sinensis   Legume Family

Black-eyed peas (mainly a Southern dish), table cow peas, crowder peas, and their near-relative, the asparagus-pea, are among the legumes highest in protein, and a mainstay of African nutrition. Nearer beans than peas botanically, these are easy to grow; the shelled seeds may be prepared green or pods may be allowed to cure on the vines for dried "peas." They're intolerant of chill, plant black-eyed peas only when the soil is quite warm. It helps to use a bacterial inoculum to trigger off nitrogen fixation in the roots—be sure to buy the appropriate inoculum for *Vigna*. If you never have grown this vegetable, try it in a hot, sunny corner of the garden. Spade in spent plants for great soil improvement.

Soil Preparation

Deeply dug, moderately fertile, high-humus soil gives the best results. Dress the cow-pea area with old rotted manure or finished compost, 3 to 4 bushels per 100 square feet, and turn the soil as deeply as possible. Top-dress with 1 pound per 100 square feet of 2–10–10 fertilizer at planting time and rake it in.

Planting

Open drills about 3 inches deep on 2-foot centers and sow three to four peas per foot; cover with 1 inch of loose soil and trod down.

Cultivation and Management

When seedlings have several true leaves, thin to 9 to 12 inches. Cultivate frequently and deeply with a pronged cultivator; well-aerated soil gives strongest plants. Water only when soil is quite dry, then soak deeply. Pick some pods when seeds are fully grown but still green and use for the table and for canning or freezing; allow the last of the crop to dry on the plant to be shelled for dried peas.

Pests and Diseases

Pests are the same as for beans; watch especially for aphids and Mexican bean beetle; apply diazinon, malathion, or for the beetle, Dylox.

Black-Eyed Pea Cultivars

Black-Eyed Pea, 65 days; 20-inch bushes with many 10-inch pods filled with small, cream-colored, black-eyed seeds.

Brown Crowder, 70 days; 24-inch bushes, 12-inch pods with pale peas that turn brown when cooked.

California Blackeye, 75 days; vigorous, 20-inch plants, resist wilt and nematodes, 8-inch pods filled with probably the best quality of all black-eyed peas.

Extra Early Black Eye, 50 days; semi-dwarf plants with very large crop of good-quality pods; a good strain to grow in short Northern summers.

Tendersweet Black Eye, 70 days; 28-inch bushes with huge crops of 12-inch pods filled with top-quality peas.

White Crowder, like *Brown Crowder,* only peas stay cream-colored when cooked.

White Lady, 75 days; 24-inch bushes with large crops of pods with small green peas. A fine sort to dry.

Note: If your garden soil is heavy and uncooperative so that spring crops are sparse and summer crops begin to fail, work up the soil as best you can and plant a dense stand of cow peas or soybeans. When the plants are fully grown, chop them down and spade then under. This "green manure" treatment can convert the worst soil into garden soil if used frequently.

Sugar Peas

Pisum sativum var. *saccharatum*   Legume Family

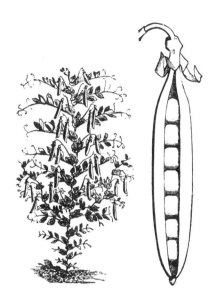

These are the garden peas grown to be eaten pod and all. Grow and maintain them just as you would other garden peas, but plant them as early as possible as they tolerate no warm, humid weather. In fact, they are most temperamental, yielding only moderate crops of pods under the best of conditions, but because they are absolutely delicious, and essential to some cookery, grow them if you can afford the space. The vines will be gone in time to set tomato, eggplant, or pepper plants where they grew.

Cultivars

Dwarf Gray Seeded, 70 days; pods large and choice; plant only in cool climate.

Little Sweetie, 60 days; 16-inch plants, 2½-inch pods. Excellent quality.

Mammoth Melting Sugar, 68 days; 4½-foot vines, 4-inch pods; for cool climates.

Super Sweetpod, 68 days; 3-foot vines, 4½-inch pods. Must be staked. Very good.

Pepper

Capsicum annuum   Nightshade Family

Peppers are easy to grow, though most require a fairly long season. One or two plants of hot peppers usually meets the family's needs, and one green pepper plant for every two persons usually is sufficient. Peppers are related to tomatoes, eggplants, potatoes, tobacco, petunias, and other Solanaceous species. They belong in every small garden, at one sunny end out of the way, as they are very high in vitamins and useful in salads, as a vegetable, and for seasoning. They can be pickled and canned, or blanched and frozen.

Soil Preparation

Pepper plants grow best in very well-drained, deeply worked soil that is high in humus. Plant them where a heavily manured crop grew last year, or dress the soil with barnyard manure or compost, 3 to 4 bushels per 100 square feet, and spade it under, turning the soil at least 12 inches deep. Work down the bed and apply 5–10–5 fertilizer, 3 ounces per square yard, and rake it in. Go carefully with readily available forms of nitrogen around pepper plants as an excess will cause blossoms to abort and fall. Organic gardeners use only bonemeal and potash in their pepper patches.

Planting

Start pepper plants indoors about eight weeks before the frost-free date. In a flat of germinating soil, sparsely sow seeds and cover to a depth of ¼ inch. Hold at 72° to 75° F. for germination (will take about fourteen days). Pepper plants must be grown warm, day and night, and in very strong light. When they have four true leaves, transplant to small pot or space out in a flat. When the garden is thoroughly warmed, harden the plants outdoors for a few days and then move them to their permanent quarters. Mark off rows on 30-inch centers and set plants 18 to 24 inches apart. Water in with transplant (high phosphate) fertilizer.

Cultivation and Management

Peppers are warm-weather plants; but they also need

ample soil moisture. When rainfall is less than 1 inch per week, make up the difference with morning irrigation. Keep the soil shallowly stirred with a pronged cultivator. Biweekly applications of pale manure water or a low-nitrogen soluble fertilizer solution keeps plants coming on strong. If the temperature drops below 55° F., if the plants lack for soil moisture, or if the soil nitrogen level is excessively high, blossoms will fall rather than set fruit.

Pests and Diseases

Few pests and diseases attack pepper plants, though aphids and flea beetles sometimes are a problem, and if your garden is infested with corn borers or stalk borers, these will enter pepper stems with devastating results as peppers are naturally brittle. In certain areas pepper maggots and pepper weevils are destructive; where these occur, check with the County Extension Agent for local recommendations on control. Otherwise, for general pests, occasional spraying with malathion or a vegetable garden insecticide mix—always add a sticker-spreader—will keep peppers clean.

Cultivars

Sweet Peppers
Dozens of strains are available, many favored very locally. This is a selection of the better sorts.

Bell Boy, 72 days; a recent hybrid with exceptionally blocky, thick-walled fruit.

California Wonder, 75 days; exceptionally good fruit, but plants mosaic-susceptible.

Canape, 62 days; very early, F_1 hybrid; heavy yielding, smallish green fruits that turn bright red. Good home variety.

Early Niagara Giant, 65 days; moderate yields of exceptionally choice fruit; mosaic-resistant.

Emerald Giant, 74 days; thick-walled fruit on an upright plant; good quality.

Goliath, 66 days; a huge, elongated pepper, green turning red, on high-production plants. Very sweet.

Keystone Resistant Giant, 80 days; a late, mosaic-resistant sort with large yields of heavy, square fruit of prime quality; green, turns fiery red.

Lady Bell, 70 days; an early hybrid, with deep, blocky fruit of exceptional quality; green turning red, mosaic-resistant.

Pimiento, 80 days; a heart-shaped pepper, beautiful, for pickling for pimiento.

Ruby King, 69 days; large, fleshy, sweet peppers, green turning red. Old favorite.

Staddon's Select, 72 days; one of the best; generous crops of blocky, thick-fleshed peppers, mosaic-resistant. Plants are tall and somewhat brittle.

Vinedale, 62 days; for short seasons; a Canadian strain, dwarf, free-bearing, betters medium-sized, pointed, with thick flesh. Light green turning red. Easy.

Yolo Wonder, 80 days; an old standby; large crops of heavy, very meaty fruit, sweet and brittle. Mosaic-resistant.

Hot Peppers

Hot Portugal, 65 days; 6 inches long, peppers of the cayenne type, tremendous crops on upright plants. Very hot.

Hungarian Wax, 70 days; waxy, yellow, long slender fruits, hot as cayenne.

Jalapeño, 78 days; fruit small, dark-green, thick-meated, extremely pungent; used almost exclusively for pickling.

Large Red Cherry, 82 days; bushy plants bearing great numbers of flattened, round peppers under 2 inches across. Extremely hot.

Long Slim Red Cayenne, 70 days; 5-inch-long, ½-inch wide red fruits, one of the hottest. Dries easily for winter use.

Long Thick Red Cayenne, 70 days; as above, but fruits larger, thicker, and not quite so hot. Good for ketchups, chili sauces.

Red Chili, 82 days; fruits small, pointed, quite hot. Not a true chili pepper.

Tabasco, 90 days; upright plants loaded with small, slender, greenish peppers that eventually turn bright red. This one is hottest of all.

Other Peppers

Often home gardeners like to grow unusual plants, and some of the not too common peppers are among the handsomest and most usable of unusual vegetables.

Canada Cheese, 75 days; a pimiento-type, plants very productive, fruits thick-walled, firm and bright red. Mild.

Romanian, 80 days; strong plants bearing yellow, waxy fruits 4½ inches long, 2½ inches wide; flesh mild, but the ribs may be pungent unless removed.

Sweet Hungarian (Yellow Banana), 75 days; huge crops of 6-inch-long, 1½-inch-wide, thick waxy yellow peppers that are extremely mild and delicious. Turns red.

Szegedi, 70 days; similar to *Romanian,* but fruit is larger, flesh thicker. Choice.

132

Potatoes

Irish, White, or Round Potato

Solanum tuberosum   Nightshade Family

A cool-weather crop, the potato is only moderately tolerant of frost. Accordingly, the major areas of summer potato production in the United States are in the Northern states; winter production centers along the Rio Grande, in California, and Florida. Home gardeners usually try for an early summer crop grown from spring-set "seed," and those who take potato growing seriously plant another crop after mid-summer to be dug in late fall. The latter practice is especially recommended for Zone 4 through Zone 6 gardens.

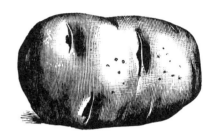

Soil Preparation

Potatoes grow best on deeply dug, porous soil, sandy loam to clay loam (tubers will be better formed on the former), that is quite fertile and well furnished with decayed organic residues. A pH of 5.4 to 6.2 is best; on neutral to alkaline soils potatoes are subject to scab disease. Never plant potatoes on recently limed soil. If possible, deeply dig potato soil in the fall, incorporating ½ bushel or more of old stable manure per square yard. Leave the soil rough over winter. If you must wait until spring to spade, complete the job as early as possible and use only very well-rotted manure. Prepare the soil for planting by broadcasting 2 to 4 ounces of 5–10–10 fertilizer per square yard (or substitute 10–10–10, using the lighter amount). Fork or rotary-till deeply. Older recommendations include placing fertilizer under the "seed" at planting time, but often this results in malformed and off-flavor tubers. It is possible to layer decayed manure below the "seed" (see below) in soil that is not of the very best.

Planting

Potato rows are spaced 24 to 36 inches apart, depending on the vigor of the variety grown and on use (crops for new potatoes are planted on the closer spacing). In the home garden, try the closer spacing—this means hand cultivation in most cases—the first time around. Open trench rows 5 to 6 inches deep and 6 inches wide; sprinkle in an inch or two of compost or old, composted manure, and cover with an inch or so of loose soil. This is the seedbed on which the potato "seed" is planted. After planting, cover seed pieces or eyes with an inch or more of soil and pat down. Sprouts should appear in twelve to twenty days.

Potatoes are grown from tubers or pieces of tubers. In America, we buy "eyes" from the mail-order seed company. These are tuber buds with a small core of tuber below. In some areas seed pieces are available; these are tuber divisions with two or three buds (eyes). For a few strains, whole, small potatoes are planted, but this is exceptional. When a potato tuber is cut into seed pieces or cored for eyes (each of these may be called a "seed") the pieces are air-dried for a few days during which time a natural layer of cork tissue develops on the cut surfaces, sealing in the succulent inner tissue. Commercial "seed" usually is treated with a fungicide after cork formation to further insure against decay of the "seed." If you cut your own seed pieces at home, let the pieces cure in a dim, cool room for a few days and then shake them, a few at a time, in a paper bag containing a small amount of a garden fungicide such as ferbam, fermate, or zineb.

Sow seed pieces in the open trench 8 to 12 inches apart, the wider spacing for heavy yielding cultivars or for potatoes grown for storage. Cover, tamp down the soil with the back of a garden rake, then rake the soil between the rows where you have walked so it is loose and will drain well.

Cultivation and Management

When potato sprouts are about 6 inches high, rake soil toward them from between the rows, making a ridge along each potato row which almost buries the shoots. Rotary-till or fork the ground between the rows. If your soil is very infertile, at this time it will help to side-dress the soil, before forking, with the same fertilizer described above, 2 ounces per square yard. In about three weeks pull up the soil again, this is the final hilling; each ridge should be a broad-based, steep-sided hill, with just the tops of the stems showing. From now on, rake the sides of the ridges, working across the row bottom to top, so germinating weed seeds are dislodged and the potato patch remains weed-free with loose soil. Potatoes are dug when the tops turn yellow and die down; usually these are pulled and taken out of the garden, then the ridges are carefully spaded open to expose the tubers which air-dry for a few hours prior to gathering. It is possible to carefully dig into the side of a potato hill, some eight or ten weeks after planting, to sneak out a few small new potatoes here and there without dislodging the plants, and entire plantings may be lifted any time new potatoes have formed, if that is your goal.

An Alternate Method of Planting and Management

Where soil drainage is slow, or soil is rocky or heavy, an alternate method of management is productive. Work up the soil as described above with manures and fertilizers. Work down the planting area in very early spring and mark out rows. For this technique, usually 24-inch centers are suitable. Stretch out a cord to indicate the row and lay out seed pieces on the surface. When the entire potato patch is seeded (soil level, "seed" on top of loose earth) cover the entire patch with at least 6 inches of loose straw. When sprouts are 6 inches high, if possible, deepen the straw by adding another generous layer. At "digging" time, simply fork away the straw and there lie the potatoes, clean, soilless, and bright-colored—on the surface of the earth! This technique is common in parts of the Midwest and in rocky portions of New England.

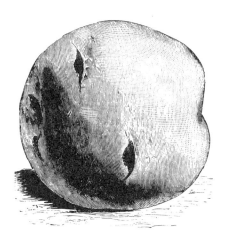

Timing for Potatoes

The earliest varieties ought to go into the ground at least two to three weeks prior to the frost-free date in your area. Throughout much of the United States St. Patrick's Day, March 17, is the traditional planting time, but in the Lower Missouri Valley early potatoes are planted shortly after St. Valentine's Day in many cases. The main crop and later maturing strains are planted two to three weeks later. The idea is for the plants to complete as much growth as possible before warm weather arrives, which puts an end to tuber development and encourages leafy top growth.

Where the summer is hot, perhaps fairly dry, and where quite a long autumn is common, usually the second crop of potatoes grows better than the first. In mid-summer, clear away a new potato patch and work up the soil as described above; if soil is very dry, wait until after a rain or else water thoroughly a day or two before deep spading, manuring, and tilling or forking. Do not set seed pieces in a wet furrow, as they will rot. Mulch in the planted potato rows to keep the sun's rays from the soil; where summers are not overly hot, omit this. Unless an unexpected frost hits succulent plants, potato plants will gradually harden as nights cool, and so will withstand several light frosts. It is possible to toss loose straw over the tops (in spring, too) if an untimely frost threatens, brushing it between the rows through

135

sunny days. Often this late crop of potatoes is of superior yield and quality.

Pests and Diseases

Potatoes are prone to several potentially devastating fungus diseases, at least one serious bacterial disease, and several destructive viruses. The first line of defense is *certified* seed pieces or "eyes" or "seed potatoes"; never rely on grocery store potatoes or on home-grown stock—only when you know *for sure* it is clean. Your County Extension Agent's office can supply data on potato diseases common in your area and on cultivars which resist these diseases. Finally, use only fungicide-treated seed pieces, eyes, or seed potatoes, because destructive fungi can be carried on these vegetative parts to infect the entire patch.

Early blight, a soil-borne fungus, appears first (usually in damp weather in early spring) as irregular black or brown dots on the leaves which quickly enlarge with concentric rings. The disease reduces leaf and stem tissue that feeds developing tubers and may destroy a crop. Late blight, usually carried on tubers left in the soil or on infected seed pieces, appears as dark, soft-looking, water-logged patches on leaves and stems; during wet weather white mold develops on these patches (usually on the undersides of leaves) and an entire planting of potato plants may go soggy and rotten in a few days. Potato dusts and sprays, usually based on Bordeaux mixture or on a copper or carbamate fungicide, control these diseases *if applied early,* before the diseases start or gain headway. As these same diseases may destroy plantings of tomatoes later in the season, it is critical to keep them out of the garden. Where spring and early summer weather is either damp from rain or humidity, make it a practice to spray or dust potatoes at one- to two-week intervals beginning with the first hilling. Verticillium wilt (often brought into the garden with infected tomato seedlings) survives in the soil; potato plants yellow, wilt, and die. Avoid planting in infected soil, work soil deeply with as much manure as possible. There is no chemical treatment for this disease. Scab, caused by a primitive fungus, roughens the skin of potato tubers with black tissue and may somewhat reduce a yield, though it does not injure the interior flesh of infected tubers. Avoid lime and plant resistant varieties if scab is a problem. Blackleg is a bacterial disease; infected young shoots rot off at the base after browning or blackening. The two substances which control this disease, both mercurials, have been taken from us by the Environmental Protection Agency, so we have to rely on good drainage (through deep cultivation) and certified "seed" as ways to avoid the disease.

Of the several viruses known, symptoms are diffuse, sometimes appearing as yellow rings on foliage, as mottling of foliage, or as abnormal, prickly leaves. These viruses are transmitted by aphids and leafhoppers, which have to be controlled. They may originate from poor "seed" or from nearby virus reservoir species, such as the native pokeweed plant. Certified seed pieces should yield virus-free plants.

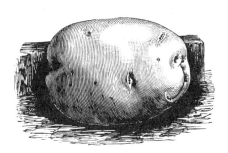

Aphids and leafhoppers seldom build up sufficient populations on potato plants to be a real problem, but because they transmit devastating diseases they should be controlled. Commercial potato dusts and sprays include good control chemicals, or spray as necessary with diazinon or a nicotine-sulfate preparation. Colorado potato beetle larvae can quickly defoliate a potato patch; the ugly yellowish orange, somewhat pudgy, soft larvae creep about on the leaves, chewing away; adult beetles are roundish, striped yellow and black. Control these with methoxychlor or with a rotenone or pyrethrum preparation. The same chemicals serve to control the tiny, active, shining brown or black flea beetles which chew small round holes in leaves. Potato tubers may be ruined by tunnels eaten out by wireworms in the soil; until the E.P.A. regulations banned the use, five percent chlordane dust tilled through the soil at planting time served as a very satisfactory control. Today we have to make do with tunneled potatoes.

Cultivars

American potatoes, today, are white-fleshed, some rather crisp, others, notably the **Idaho Russet** and its relatives, are mealy or floury. The crisp-fleshed potatoes are used for steaming or boiling, the floury ones for baking. Years ago the extremely succulent but low-yielding potatoes called "yellow potatoes" were available, but no longer. These had a distinctly yellowish flesh when raw, and the crisp yellow ones—still widely grown in Europe—were the very finest thing for potato salad, either cold or hot.

Anoka, early, smooth-skinned white, round tubers; good flavor.

Bake King, early; from Cornell University, a new Russet type of superb quality, though of moderate yield.

Chippewa, early, roundish, smooth, pale sand-colored skin.

Green Mountain, mid-season, large, pale rust-colored, flat, oblong tubers.

Irish Cobbler, extra-early, white-skinned, rough and nubby but high quality; not very disease-resistant.

Katahdin, late, smooth, round tuber, white-skinned, best on light soil, considerable disease resistance.

Kennebec, late, smooth white tuber, blight- and mosaic-resistant, good quality.

Norchip, early, a smooth, floury, white-skinned potato with shallow eyes.

Norgold Russet, early, a brownish-skinned Russet, smooth, oblong tubers, floury, for baking; scab-resistant.

Norland, early, red-skinned, a smooth, shallow-eyed tuber, scab-resistant.

Red Pontiac, late, heavy yielding, smooth-skinned tuber for boiling.

Warba, early, smooth, white-skinned tuber, tolerant of mosaic.

Sweet Potato

Ipomoea batatas   Morning Glory Family

The sweet potato is not known in the wild in North America but primitive peoples throughout equatorial regions apparently always have grown it. Do not confuse the orange- to yellow-fleshed sweet potato with the true yam of the *Dioscorea* species. American gardeners know the Chinese Yam, *D. batatas*, as the ornamental Cinnamon-vine, hardy throughout Zone 5. Sweet potatoes are a Southern crop, developing over a long season, with a vine-spread of 6 feet or so. They are not usually grown in small home gardens as they are not only space-consuming, but also occupy their area for most of the growing season. It is possible to set a few plants toward one side of the garden after an early crop of leaf lettuce.

Soil Preparation

Sweet potatoes grow best on the light-textured red soils extending from Oklahoma through southern Missouri, Indiana, and as far north as New Jersey, as well as throughout most of the South. But they will grow in almost any very well-fertilized neutral soil. Dig the sweet potato area deeply in the fall, incorporating as much as a 3-inch layer of old barnyard manure or compost. In spring, at planting time, top-dress the soil with 2 ounces per square yard of 5–10–5 fertilizer and fork deeply. Mark out rows on at least 3-foot centers (more room is better) and rake the soil into broad ridges.

Planting

Sweet potatoes always are grown from young plants which are rooted shoots pulled from buried tubers. Most growers buy their plants—mail-order sources are common—but you can start your own by burying well-budded sweet potatoes, "blind" end downward, in sand, in a hotbed. Set in the young plants (usually about 9 inches high) only when the soil is quite warm; open a trench along the top of the long shallow ridge and set rooted cuttings 3 or 4 inches deep on 15- to 24-inch centers, depending on the productivity of your soil. Water plants in with a transplant fertilizer for best results.

Cultivation and Management

Sweet potatoes always are grown in clean cultivation as they need the sun-warmed soil. As plants resume growth gradually rake more soil toward them, raising the ridge. Sweet potatoes are a low-maintenance crop; simply keep the weeds down and irrigate only through periods of severe drought, as they can withstand considerable dry weather if the soil was deeply worked previous to planting. Avoid summer fertilizing as this encourages leafy growth at the expense of the tuberous roots.

As vines yellow and shed leaves due to cold weather, or are lightly frosted, cut them away immediately. Let the sweet potatoes cure in the soil for a few days, then dig them (take care not to injure the tubers as they decay readily at this stage) and wash them clean *and air-dry on screens in a warm, dry, place.* When the tuberous roots are quite dry outside, store in a warm, dry, rather airless place.

Pests and Diseases

Usually there is no problem with sweet potatoes in the home garden. Occasionally in the South the sweet potato weevil (a black, red, and blue snout beetle) chews the foliage, and tortoise beetles may become a pest. Methoxychlor, Dylox, or old-fashioned arsenate of lead control these readily; spray, and use a sticker-spreader as dusts and plain spray solution fail to coat the leaves. Diseases are almost unknown.

Cultivars

The sweet potato cultivar picture has changed radically in recent years; for decades growers stuck with various "Puerto Rico" strains called "yams" and with very fine and not so very fine strains with the words New Jersey in the name. *Nancy Hall* was another long-time favorite. Today, look for newer sorts such as:

All Golds, with medium-sized tuberous roots of high quality, fiberless, deep gold-orange flesh of fine flavor. A good Midwestern sort.

Centennial, very smooth, rather reddish sweet potatoes with dark-orange, fiber-free flesh; a high yielder of top quality, and not too demanding of soil type.

Georgia Reds, a high-yielding, long-season sort producing huge harvests of purplish-red sweet potatoes with rich orange flesh of excellent quality. This is not a sort for northern growing, but excellent south of St. Louis.

Vineless Puerto Rico, a southern, long-season strain that takes up little space because the vines are short and bushy. The sweet potatoes are somewhat fibrous; good tasting but not comparable to the above three strains.

Pumpkin

Cucurbita pepo   Cucumber Family

Pumpkins, as a rule, do not fit well into the home garden because the long, running plants take up too much room. However, they grow perfectly well on a fence or trellis (a husky "vine" can carry a 20-pound pumpkin easily) and at least one bush sort now is available. Pumpkins are closely allied to the small yellow gourds and to the giant crookneck (Cushaw) squashes, so these should not be grown with pumpkins in the garden. There is no problem with cucumbers or other melons. Pumpkins, like squashes, are heavy users of nutrients and water. For culture, *see* Squash.

Cultivars

Big Max, really a hybrid or selection of the Hungarian squash, this is a pinkish-orange pumpkin to 200 pounds or more on runners 80 to 100 feet long.

Cinderella, 105 days; *the only bush pumpkin;* 10-inch diameter, round, orange pumpkins at about 7 pounds each. Plant in hills with a 2 × 3-foot spacing.

Connecticut Field, 115 days; this is the 15- to 20-pound Hallowe'en pumpkin, wonderful for the kids, grows on the fence, not overly edible.

Jack O'Lantern, 110 days; a rather cylindrical, small, deep-orange pumpkin for decorative purposes. Good fence climber.

King of Giants, 120 days; huge, pinkish-orange, round pumpkins, for Hallowe'en—where a 200-pound Jack O'Lantern is wanted!

Large Cheese, 110 days; a round, flat pumpkin, meaty and sweet, buff-colored. Good keeper. Grows 20 to 30 pounds.

Small Sugar, 115 days; a fine pie-type, 7 pounds, globe; deep-orange pumpkins. Excellent.

Spookie, 110 days; an improved sort of the above, smaller, excellent home variety.

Radish

Raphanus sativus   Mustard Family

Common table radishes, both globe and icicle forms, derive from European ancestry; less familiar is *R. sativus longipinnatus*, commonly grown in China and usually cooked. These giant radishes may attain as much as 50 pounds; they require a long, cool growing season.

The secret to tender, succulent radishes is quick growth. Radishes grown slowly are pithy and hot, scarcely palatable. Grow radishes throughout winter in a frost-free frame, sow in the open garden when soil becomes workable and again in late summer for crops during the cool fall weather. Radishes are among the easiest of crops; the windowsill gardener can grow them in a deep flat. While most Americans know them as "finger food" and as a choice additive to the mixed salad, they also can be steamed tender to be dressed with butter or a sauce as a cooked vegetable, and they are ideal to eat raw, sliced paper thin, and stacked on freshly buttered bread as tea sandwiches.

Soil Preparation

Any friable garden loam will grow a good crop of radishes. The soil should be moderately rich, well spaded, and of uniform consistency (no layers) to a depth of at least 12 inches for best roots. While a reasonably high organic fraction is desirable, do not plant radishes on freshly manured soil. Constant soil moisture makes all the difference, especially when the temperature is above 70° F.

Planting

The planting season begins outdoors when soil is frost-free and workable. Mark off drills 12 inches apart and open them to a depth of ½ inch. Sow seeds two or three per inch and cover ⅓ inch deep; lightly pat down soil with the back of the rake. Seeds usually germinate in four to five days, slightly longer for some of the icicle sorts. The crop is ready to harvest in twenty-five to forty days; therefore, make successive plantings once each week rather than one large planting. Plant for fall use, and if you have a deep frame, plant radishes (with lettuce) for late fall and early winter use. Radishes may be interplanted with slow-germinating crops; this is a handy way to mark rows of parsnips, carrots, beets, and similar vegetables with rather weak seedlings. The radish seedlings tend to break crusted soil so other seedlings can come through, and they identify the row clearly. For inter-planting, sow not more than one radish seed per inch or their spreading leaves may crowd out the main crop.

Cultivation and Management

The radish bed should be kept loose and open at all times. As quickly as soil is workable after each rain or after watering, with a small hoe or pronged cultivator scratch the soil to break the crust. Work as closely as possible to the radish plants as loose soil tends to encourage rapid growth. As soon as globe or oval sorts are a reasonable size begin to pull for the table, thinning the stand so remaining plants can grow quickly. Do likewise for the icicle sorts; roots the size of your little finger are crisp and delicious.

Pests and Diseases

A few fungi may attack radishes, notably leaf mildew, but usually are not worth treating. In wet years you may have to resort to spraying with an approved vegetable fungicide or apply an all-purpose vegetable spray or dust. The trouble is, you have to get there before the disease because control chemicals do not eradi-cate the problem. If leaf fungi are a problem, begin treating plants when the first true leaves appear and re-treat twice weekly until plants are nearly table-ready. A worse scourge is the flea beetle, which riddles the radish leaves with tiny holes. Dylox will control this insect, or use an all-purpose vegetable garden spray or dust which contains rotenone or pyrethrum. Where root worms are a problem, treat the soil deeply a month before plant-ing with a soil fumigant as cleared for use in your area by your State University Department of Entomology. The County Extension Agent will know about this.

Cultivars

Table Radish Strains
Cavalier, 21 days; globe-shaped red, white interior, a truck gardener's strain for growing on muckland.
Champion, 20 to 26 days; globe-shaped, solid bright red exterior, pure white inside. Choice.
Cherry Belle, 24 days; probably the most familiar grocery store radish; red globe with white interior. Good to fair, depend-

ing on seed source.

Crimson Giant, 29 days; oval, scarlet root growing to 2 inches in diameter in fertile, damp soil.

French Breakfast, 25 days; oval, scarlet with white tip, a superior sort for home production.

Icicle (also called *White Icicle*), 30 days; crisp, white flesh; roots 4 to 5 inches long; requires rich, friable soil. Choice.

Perfection White Tip, 26 days; globe-shaped, scarlet above, lower half pure white, mild, tender.

Radar, 18 days; very early, scarlet globe. Good table sort.

Red Boy, 22 days; a refined strain from *Scarlet Globe,* oval, scarlet; a commercial strain.

Red Prince Improved, 24 days; another *Scarlet Globe* relative, this one tolerant of fusarium fungus.

Saxa Elite, 21 days; a European strain, red globe shape, for early spring or fall sowing; choice.

Scarlet Globe Special, 23 days; a standard market sort, roots scarlet, globe-shaped, uniform.

Summer Cross, 45 days; a strange Japanese hybrid, bringing the winter radish into summer culture. These white, icicle-shaped radishes are ready when an inch thick, six inches long, but will continue through cool fall weather to 1 foot long, 2½ inches thick, still tasty. Good for late August sowing.

White Ball, 25 days; one of several pure white, globe-shaped radishes; flesh crisp and sweet. Choice.

Winter (Giant) Radishes

Chinese Rose, 55 days; a round, rose-colored radish for fall planting that grows to enormous proportions.

Chinese White, 55 days; a long, thick, white root; good, but for home use I recommend *Summer Cross* described above.

Round Black Spanish, 55 days; a round, black-skinned radish that is rather pungent; grows to quite a large size.

Rhubarb

Rheum rhaponticum   Buckwheat Family

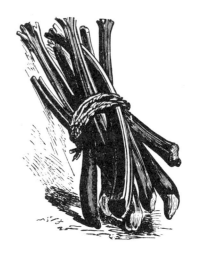

We know that rhubarb was in cultivation in China 3,000 years ago, and has been in Western gardens for a very long time. It is a long-lived perennial. Prepare your rhubarb bed outside the vegetable garden as it will interfere with normal cultivation. In fact, a solid recommendation is for the preparation of a special bed to house rhubarb, asparagus, horseradish, Jerusalem artichoke, and any other perennials as all have the same general exposure (full sun) requirements and soil needs.

Soil Preparation

As rhubarb will stand for years, work the soil deeply before planting. Fast-draining, very deep, high-humus loam is best. Double-dig your bed, working great quantities of well-rotted barnyard manure or manure-enriched compost into the lower level as well as the upper spit of soil. At planting time, dress the bed with 5 ounces per square yard of 5–10–5 fertilizer or apply 4 ounces of bonemeal, 2 ounces of hoof meal, and 1 ounce of potash. Fork through the top 6 inches.

Planting

An easy way is to buy fresh, unshriveled roots from a reliable dealer. In early spring set these 1 to 2 inches deep, depending on the heaviness of the soil. Water them in, and mulch deeply with loose straw until the weather is completely settled. Normal spacing is 3- to 4-foot centers each way. To grow rhubarb from seed, start in a flat with any suitable germinating compost; cover seed to a depth of ¼ inch. When they are ready to transplant to the open ground, set them in 4 inches apart, in nursery rows on 12-inch centers for the first year. One year later, move select plants to their permanent growing site.

Cultivation and Management

Never gather stalks from the first-year set plants, and only a few from plants two years in the garden. After that, leaves may be pulled freely, but each plant must be allowed to mature a reasonable number of leaves to feed the rhizome for the following season. To harvest leaves, grasp the stalk firmly near the base and pull with a steady upward and outward pressure. Do not *cut* leaves as stubs decay and may rot the rhizome. Keep rhubarb in clean cultivation and water frequently through dry weather. The very finest stalks come from plants pushed into vigorous growth with free use of tea-colored manure water applied almost daily early in the season.

In the autumn, mulch the clumps with a generous heap of old barnyard manure or rich compost after frost has blackened the foliage. Some growers apply a slow-acting fertilizer in late summer to strengthen plants before winter. In the North, top the manure mulch with evergreen boughs after frost is in the soil.

Every five or six years lift rhubarb, divide, and reset. If you have several plants, stagger the planting times so you always have ample leaves to harvest.

Always cut out flower stalks as they appear deep in the plant. Plenty of manure and water will keep fruiting to a minimum, but a plant allowed to flower is seriously weakened and will not be a good leaf producer for some time.

You can force tender, bleached rhubarb early in the year. Obtain a wooden nail keg or a large clay tile—either with a removable cap. Pull mulch from the crown of the plant in March and set the container over it, capped. Mound around with several bushels of hot horse manure or hot compost. As heat reaches the plant, long, pale leaf-stalks will reach upwards in the container. These can be harvested a few at a time for early rhubarb. Do not uncover all at once when weather is mild, but leave the cap off for a few days, then take the barrel or tile away, and scatter the manure or compost.

Cultivars

Most commercial strains are good quality and similar; *Victoria* is mild, green-stalked; **Cherry Red, Chipman Red, MacDonald,** and **Valentine** all are red and of superior quality. **Ruby** and **Strawberry** are red, small-stalked, weak.

Rutabaga (Swede)

Brassica napobrassica   Mustard Family

Rutabaga, or swede, is a cool-weather crop, an excellent garden crop for the northern climates. In warmer climates, sow seed July 1 or later; roots will not grow to full size, but at least a crop will mature through the cool fall months. Closely akin to turnips, rutabagas grow similarly.

Soil Preparation

Sandy loam to loam is best; any soil, very heavily manured the previous season, will produce a respectable crop. As these are gross feeders and demand much moisture, deeply worked soil, high in humus and freely enriched with mineral fertilizer just prior to planting time, gives best results. Never plant rutabagas on freshly manured ground.

Planting

Mark off rows on 2- to 3-foot centers and open drills 1 inch deep. Sow two or three seeds per inch. Early in the year when the soil is moisture-laden, cover seeds with ¼ inch of pulverized soil; later plantings are covered with ½ inch of soil. When seedlings are well developed, work the soil level around them. When leaves are 4 to 5 inches high, thin seedlings to stand 1 foot apart for early plantings; 6 to 8 inches apart for later plantings.

Cultivation and Management

Grow rutabagas in clean cultivation; with a scuffle hoe, work the soil frequently, maintaining a dust mulch right up to the plants. If rain is insufficient to keep soil damp 2 or 3 inches down, water thoroughly. If soil is reasonably fertile at planting time, no additional fertilizer is required, but if plants seem to lag, water generously with tea-colored liquid manure solution or with any other high phosphate liquid fertilizer.

Pests and Diseases

Pests and diseases which attack the cabbage and turnip

also attack rutabaga, but often do not do much damage. Spray or dust young plants with diazinon or rotenone when necessary to protect them from leaf-eating beetles and other insects. Avoid planting rutabagas where cabbages or turnips have grown for two or three years so risk of club root disease is diminished.

Rarely, rutabagas develop an internal tissue breakdown known as brown heart or water core; this is due to a deficiency of boron in the soil. A single application of fertilizer with trace elements usually takes care of this for years, or foliage may be sprayed with an extremely dilute solution of borax water.

Cultivars

Altasweet, 92 days; deep yellow flesh, ultra-sweet hybrid; highly recommended.

American Purple Top, 90 days; pale yellow flesh, standard, old variety. Good.

Laurentian, 90 days; pale yellow flesh; Canada's leading commercial strain. Stores well.

Macomber, 92 days; a large, white-fleshed rutabaga; standard, old variety. Choice.

Superba, 74 days; an early New England strain; yellow, sweet.

York Swede, 90 days; a Laurentian strain, grown where club root is a problem.

Salsify (Oyster Plant)

Tragopogon porrifolius   Composite Family
Also Black Salsify *(Scorzonera)* and
Spanish Salsify *(Scolymus hispanica)*

Salsify (and its close relatives) are ancient root crops; the oyster plant is the commonest, but *Scorzonera* is tastier. These plants are biennials, seeded in the spring to grow throughout summer (keep them at one end of the garden as space will be tied up throughout the season) to be dug up in fall for use. Or leave roots in the soil to be dug through winter and spring. Plants will bloom the following year (don't let them as seedlings are a serious problem) and die. The roots of the salsifies are long, rather ropy looking; but when steamed tender and buttered or creamed they are delicious; often steamed pieces of common salsify are breaded and fried as "false oysters."

Soil Preparation

A light loam gives best results, but heavier soils may be lightened with very large amounts of old manure or compost spaded into the top 14 inches. Deep soil preparation is essential to production of thick, straight roots. Before seeding, fork in deeply 5–10–5 fertilizer at the rate of 5 ounces per square yard. As organic gardeners favor these crops, they will use a combination of 3 ounces bonemeal, 1 ounce of hoof meal, and 1 ounce of potash. Rotary tilling to mix these fertilizers deeply through the soil gives better results.

Planting

Open shallow drills on 15- to 24-inch centers; sow seeds two or three per inch and thin to 3 inches apart. When young plants are 4 inches high, lightly side-dress with 2 ounces of 5–10–5 fertilizer per yard.

Cultivation and Management

Grow all the salsifies in clean cultivation; water generously during prolonged drought—water should soak 15 inches into the soil. The crop needs no other special attention.

Cultivars

Mammoth Sandwich Island, 115 days; roots 8 inches long, 1 to 1½ inches thick at the shoulder, smooth and dull white.

Scorzonera (Black Salsify), 115 days; similar to the above, but roots larger and of better flavor; skin black, flesh white.

Spanish Salsify (Scolymus hispanica), 115 days; is much like Black Salsify; in Europe young shoots are eaten as cardoons, and flowers are used to adulterate saffron.

Shallot

Allium ascalonicum   Lily Family

Not very hardy, shallots are the bane of gardeners as they are difficult to grow, and the delight of cooks who favor their sweetish, mild, onion-like flavor. Shallots almost never form seed but are grown from separated divisions of the bulb. Prepare soil deeply as for onions; and cultivate and manage the crop the same way, that is, clean cultivation, frequent hoeing. In the South, plant in mid-winter and lift in mid-summer as the foliage dries off; further north, plant when weather is favorable (light frost is permissible, but not freezing weather). Carry over through winter indoors in a dry, frost-free place.

Planting

Divisions of the bulb remain attached at the bottom. To plant, pull divisions apart and let them dry for a day or two. Open a trench about 3 inches deep and rake full of loose, fluffy soil. Plant the divisions by shoving them halfway into the soil (never cover the tops) on 6-inch centers, rows 15 to 18 inches apart. Grow in clean cultivation always, lift when leaves dry, cure in the garden for a few days, then for ten days in an airy, shady shed. Store loose.

Spinach

Spinacia oleracea   Goosefoot Family

Spinach is the leading potherb crop in America; easy to grow, quick to mature, and with bountiful yields in a small area. Spinach makes an ideal crop for the home garden. It thrives in cool weather but fails during mid-summer heat. For best results, sow spinach in early spring, three or four weeks before the frost-free date, and again in late summer for a fall and early winter crop. From Zone V southward a fall crop may be deeply mulched with straw to provide spinach early in the spring.

Soil Preparation

Spinach demands neutral soil; have your soil tested and make the necessary adjustment to bring it between a pH of 6.0–7.0. The best results will be on sandy or silt loams, but any soil very heavily manured or fluffed up with compost tilled in deeply will produce good spinach plants. Ample fertilizer is essential; a week or so before sowing seed, till into the top few inches as much as 30 pounds per 1,000 square feet of 5–10–10 (or 5–10–5) fertilizer. Organic gardeners will use, per square yard, 4 ounces of bonemeal, 2 ounces of hoof meal, and 1 ounce of potash.

Planting

Spinach may be sown broadcast or in rows. I prefer a compromise. For rows, open 1-inch-deep drills on 1-foot centers. Scatter seeds sparsely, and as plants grow, thin to stand 4 inches apart (young plants pulled to thin may be washed and cooked whole). For broadcast growing, scatter seed sparingly and rake it into the top inch of soil, then tamp down fairly firmly. Or mark off rows on 18-inch centers, and with a 6-inch-wide hoe, skim out a 1-inch-deep, flat-bottomed trench; broadcast seed very sparsely over this and replace the soil. These broadcast rows produce a lot of vegetable and are easy to maintain. Spinach seed germinates best at 40° F.

Cultivation and Management

When seedlings have 4 to 5 leaves, fertilize generously with nitrate of soda, ammonium nitrate, or strong manure water.

Apply 3 to 6 ounces of fertilizer per yard of row, along each side of the row; water in. If fertilizer is broadcast over scattered plants, hose the crop thoroughly to wash it off. Keep spinach in clean cultivation and maintain loose soil with frequent hoeing.

Pests and Diseases

Few pests and diseases disfigure spinach; if aphids show up, spray or dust immediately with a malathion preparation. Mildews and leafspots sometimes occur during dank weather; but spraying or dusting is not recommended. Rather, plant a resistant variety. Viruses may be a problem if your garden is in a weedy, buggy environment; a clean lawn around the vegetable patch helps.

Cultivars

America, 50 days; one of the most delicious, productive, and long-standing strains, with large, crumpled leaves. Excellent quality, my main crop.

Big Crop, 40 days; a spring strain, extremely heavy crop of huge, top-quality leaves; stands well into the summer.

Bloomsdale, 39 days; a thick-leaved, very crumpled spinach favored by truck growers as it ships well. Taste is only mediocre, leaves hard to clean. Almost any other spinach is better for home gardening.

Nobel, 50 days; an old standby strain for those who prefer smooth leaves; not among the best.

Viking, 46 days; fairly smooth leaves, a good spring crop for home growing.

Virginia Savoy Blight Resistant, 39 days; a 'Bloomsdale' type for areas where blight is a problem.

Winter Bloomsdale, 45 days; a heavily crumpled, thick-leaved spinach that tolerates cold weather and stands reasonably well into heat. Good.

New Zealand Spinach

Tetragonia expansa   Carpetweed Family

This rather succulent, low, bushy plant, which is no relative of spinach, is grown for its tender young stems and leaves which are prepared as spinach; the flavor is different, less tasty according to most people, and more apt to be stringy. Its one good feature is an ability to withstand considerable summer heat.

Soil Preparation

See Spinach, page 152.

Planting, Management and Cultivation

Can be sown directly, but germination may be uneven. A better method is to soak seeds for 24 hours, then sow; three seeds per 3-inch pot of rich germinating compost. Grow on, thinned to one plant per pot, in a cool and bright area. Move to the open garden when danger of frost is past. Water in with transplant fertilizer or liquid manure. Space plants as much as 2 feet each way and pinch (use leafy tips for food) frequently to develop broad, dense bushes.

Keep New Zealand spinach in clean cultivation for insect-free, clean foliage.

Cultivars

There is just the species.

Squash

Cucurbita pepo, C. moschata, and others   Cucumber family

You have only to read the technical literature to quickly understand that scientists are not at all sure of the botanical affiliations of today's garden squashes. Indeed, the British group many of them under the heading "gourds" and refer to the rest as vegetable marrows. They don't face up to the winter squashes at all. Squashes are marvelous vegetables; the summer ones go from the garden to the table with little or no preparation—or they may be concocted into gourmet dishes. The winter squashes go from the garden into chilly storage to be used, again with little preparation, as a high-vitamin, delicious winter vegetable. No freezing, no canning, just easy preparation, good eating. Of course, there is a catch. Many of the squashes grow only in a sprawling, trailing ("vine") form, totally unsuitable for the small garden. With effort, some of these may be made to produce on a trellis, all will grow well on the compost heap, but by and large, the trailing sorts are unsuitable for a smallish garden. The bush types are something else, these are often extremely productive; one or two hills will feed several people. Today several summer squashes come as bush-types and two or three delicious winter types are now available in bush form. Grow lots of squashes; you will come to love them.

Soil Preparation

Squashes are gross feeders and they consume vast amounts of water. Their roots run deeply and over a wide area, so soil preparation must be thorough. Dress the squash area with 5 bushels of well-rotted manure per 100 square feet and spade this in, digging to a depth of 12 inches or more. Then dress the garden with 3 pounds per 100 square yards of 5–10–5 fertilizer. Mark out hills or rows, scatter a few shovelfuls of compost or old manure at each point, and fork it in. To make watering easy, sink a perforated 3-pound coffee can at each planting site, and plant three or four seeds around this reservoir. Always wait to plant squashes until the soil is quite warm and the summer weather settled in. It is possible to start squash plants early, indoors, by sowing seeds in pairs (later destroy one plant of each pair) in individual pots set in a bright, warm window, but usually little is gained by this except in cold, clammy climates. Direct sowing is best.

Planting

Cover squash seeds with ½ inch of crumbled soil. If soil is not fairly damp, open a saucer-sized planting area for each sowing site, dampen this patch of earth repeatedly, lay the seeds on the mud, and cover them with crumbly, dry soil. Capillary action will move the moisture up to the seeds. Bush-type squashes go in hills 4 feet apart each way, two or three plants per hill, and trailing sorts go in hills on 8-foot centers.

Cultivation and Management

Cultivate squash seedlings frequently so no competing weeds develop. When plants have four or five leaves, side-dress with a handful of ammonium nitrate per hill, scattered several inches from the plants and scratched in. Crowded plants do poorly; thin to two to four plants per hill.

Pests and Diseases

Various insect pests and diseases attack squash plants and an entire planting may be lost almost overnight if you fail to take proper precautions. Refer to pests and diseases of cucumbers; apply the same chemicals for the same pests.

Most people fail with summer squash because they fail to pick them early enough. Take a cue from the Italians; they bring succulent young zucchinis and some other summer squash to market with the open blossom attached. Buyers batter-dip and fry the blossoms for lunch and eat the squash for supper. Never allow a summer squash to go more than three or four days past blooming before harvest. True, they will grow and grow, to immense proportions, and at that stage they are tasteless and tough.

Cultivars

Summer Types
Often seed houses prefix cultivars named below with "early" or "baby." Zucchini strains=Cocozelle strains.
Casserta, 50 days; bush-type, cylindrical, pale green striped dark green.
Diplomat, 48 days; bush-type zucchini, very dark all-over green.

156

Greyzini, 50 days; as above, but gray-green. Superb quality.

Goldzini, 50 days; a butter-yellow zucchini, new. Also known as *Eldorado.* Good quality.

Zucchini, 47 days; dark green, flecked, cylinder; comes in several selections as *Chefzini, Black Jack* and *Black Zucchini,* all very similar. Buy a mildew-resistant strain.

Vegetable Marrow, 70 days; a bush that produces thickened, cylindrical squashes, snow white and highly regarded in England, but actually quite tasteless.

Butter Strains

Crookneck, 50 days; bush-type, bears butter-yellow, crooked, warted squashes. Good.

Golden Girl, 50 days; a hybrid of the above, straight, thickened form, Excellent.

Seneca Prolific, 52 days; first hybrid, an improvement over *Crookneck,* Excellent.

Straightneck, 52 days; very similar to *Crookneck,* but squash is straight.

Courgettes

(*Note:* always pick these when 2 inches across or smaller.)

Patty Pan (White Bush), 55 days; a flattened, scalloped bush-type squash. Seldom appreciated because growers allow fruits to turn white and develop hard white rind. Pick early, steam tender, serve with drawn butter. The best!

Winter Types
Delicious Strains

Golden Delicious, 100 days; vining, deep orange, heart-shaped fruit to 10 pounds, developed for high-vitamin baby food. Very good.

Green Delicious, 105 days; as above, but green rind, orange flesh. Splendid for freezing.

Acorn (Des Moines) Strains

Royal Queen, 90 days; as *Table Queen* but about ⅓ larger. Keeps well.

Table King, 80 days; bush-type plant bearing typical acorn squashes of the *Table Queen* sort; not quite as perfect as *Table Queen,* but very fine.

Table Queen, 85 days; a superior, vining winter squash,

bears black-green, ribbed, acorn-shaped fruits about 5 inches long. Extremely good quality.

Hubbard Strains

Baby Hubbard (Kitchenette), 100 days; vining type, fruits as **Green Hubbard** but much smaller. Fine quality.

Blue Hubbard, 110 days; vining, huge, spindle-shaped blue-green fruits, 15 to 40 pounds. Stores well but flesh not too fine-grained.

Chicago Hubbard, 115 days; similar to **Blue Hubbard,** but rind dark green, as large or larger, varies in quality.

Golden Hubbard, 90 days; vining, rich orange rind, 8- to 10-pound fruit, keeps well.

Green Hubbard (several strains of this are available), 120 days; vining, spindle-shaped, warted green rind, flesh thick yellowish-orange, dry and quite sweet. Perhaps the best of the Hubbards.

Warted Hubbard, 110 days; similar to **Green Hubbard,** but more heavily warted; flesh orange, dry, not stringy but not overly succulent. Best winter keeper.

Other Winter Types

Delicata (Sweet Potato), 100 days; vining, fruits oblong, 6 to 8 inches, cream-colored with green stripes; keeps well. Good.

Buttercup, 90 days; vining, 3- to 4-pound squat-cylindrical fruit; fine, dark orange flesh; one of the best. Stores very well.

Butternut (also strains such as **Waltham Butternut**), 55 days; club-shaped fruits, thickened neck, balled end. Buff rind, orange, dry, sweet, fine-textured meat. All are superior. Vines are rampant.

Emerald, 85 days; a new, bush-type squash with **Buttercup** fruits. Choice.

Golden Nugget, 95 days; bush-type, rock-hard, ribbed, nearly ball-shaped red-orange fruits with absolutely superb dry, fine-grained, sweet flesh. Keeps moderately well.

Hungarian Mammoth, 120 days; ribbed, ball to elongated globe, to 250 pounds or more, green, gray, blue, or orange rind, orange flesh. Amazing! Rampant.

Kindred, 80 days; As **Buttercup,** but fruits smaller (3¼ pounds) and bright orange.

Perfection, 85 days; a development of **Buttercup** without the "turban" end which wastes flesh. Extremely fine quality. Sweet.

Tomato

Lycopersicon esculentum   Nightshade Family

Tomatoes are everybody's crop. No tinned or market tomato ever compared with a fresh-picked tomato, sun-warmed from the garden. Indeed, a tomato seems best when eaten, juice dripping, right out in the vegetable patch. Experts tell us that tomatoes are nourishing, high in vitamins, minerals, and organic acids. But surely we all grow tomatoes because they are so delicious! Tomato plants grow in various soils, in various exposures, and under a number of different methods of cultivation. And yet there is a "best" way; study the recommendations. If you cannot follow them exactly, adapt them to your particular situation. You will be pleased with increased crops.

Modern tomato cultivars mostly are selections from generations of breeding within the species *Lycopersicon esculentum*. In the 1940's, the late Dr. Clarence M. Tucker, botanist at the University of Missouri, analyzed many acquisitions of tomatoes for disease resistance and found good resistance in the currant tomato, *L. pimpinellifolium*. One particular strain from Peru transmitted near-immunity to fusarium wilt to offspring of crosses between the two species, and much of the fusarium resistance in modern strains comes from this breeding. The currant tomato, once favored for planting on trash and garbage dumps in summer because the sprawling plants camouflaged the unsightliness, is now nearly unavailable. And yet it is worth looking for; the small fruits, grown in grape- or currant-like clusters, are delicious, the plants are immune to most ills, and best of all, once you get them started volunteer seedlings usually appear year after year somewhere in the garden. The currant tomato is very productive when grown in full sun in a large hanging basket or a large pot.

Tomato cultivars used to behave in one of two manners. Either the upright shoots grew on and on throughout summer, with leaves and flower clusters produced along the stems (such continuous growth is known as "indeterminate growth" and the plants continue to flower and fruit until frost), or with others, the shoots branched and grew in leafy growth and then flower clusters appeared at the tips of all shoots, thus stopping growth (such strains are known to have "determinate growth" and all shoots flower at the same time, fruits ripen for three or four pickings, and the crop is through for the season). Indeterminate tomatoes bear over a long period, are ideal for the home garden, and ought to be staked for best results. Determinate tomatoes, primarily intended for canners where it is convenient to have a whole field of fruit ripe at one time, never are staked or pruned; many determinate tomato strains ripen very early so it is nice to have two or three plants in an odd corner to furnish early tomatoes until the main crop comes on. Learn to distinguish between determinate and indeterminate tomato plants because they are handled differently for optimum fruit production.

Soil Preparation

For the biggest, best tomatoes, the plants need absolutely full sunlight. While most soils will produce some tomatoes if well drained and fertilized, a very deeply dug bed, generously enriched with coarse compost or partially decayed strawy manure, fertilized with a special tomato-growing formulation, gives best results. Where soils tend to be acid, insure that there will be plenty of calcium by adding agricultural limestone to the proposed tomato bed in the fall or winter.

Where your tomato garden is laid out and established, dress the soil in the fall with 20 pounds of compost or barnyard manure and 6 ounces of bonemeal, 4 ounces of hoof and horn meal, and 2 ounces of potassium sulfate per square yard; spade this in. If the organic fertilizers are unavailable, spade in the manure or leaf mold in the fall to improve soil texture and in spring fork in commercial tomato fertilizer (a typical formulation is 5–10–10; thus, any fertilizer with an NPK ratio of 1:2:2 will serve as a tomato fertilizer).

New homeowners or first-time gardeners almost always start with tomato plants, and because their soil has not been worked for some years, the plants do poorly. Tomato plants must have a deep, well-prepared, well-drained root run. Proceed as follows:

If you can start in the fall, mark off the plot, spade out the topsoil to a depth of one spade blade and reserve it; cover the bottom of the bed with a deep layer of barnyard manure or compost or both, dust with superphosphate, one cupful per square yard, and fork all this in. Mix the topsoil with as much leaf mold or compost or manure as you can get, and toss it back into the bed (leave it coarse and rough). If you are an organic enthusiast, add bonemeal, hoof and horn meal, and potash as recommended above. A month later, dress with a 1-pound coffee canful of agricultural limestone per square yard; allow to settle and mellow over winter; in spring, fork lightly. When soil is warm, fork again and mark off for plants.

If you have to begin in spring or early summer, locate as

large an amount of well-rotted barnyard manure, leaf mold, or compost (you always can buy it bagged), as possible. If your soil is very tight, equal parts of the additive will be necessary. Somehow loosen the soil; around a new home you may have to use a pick-mattock or a very heavy shovel. It is best to go as deep as possible. Mix into the soil the manure, leaf mold, or compost (or all three) and organic fertilizers if you have them. Add gypsum rather than lime to supply calcium. Probably you will have to pry up and do your preliminary mixing of the soil by hand, but a rotary tiller is handy to churn and blend the loosened and admixed soil. Do not work it to powder. A spring-prepared bed ought to mellow for at least three weeks before planting time.

Planting

Two methods give good results. You can start seedlings indoors early and move plants to the garden when danger of frost is past, or else directly seed where plants are to grow when danger of frost is past. Direct seeding is becoming increasingly popular as the cost of tomato plants from a commercial source increases every year.

To start seeds indoors, count back six to eight weeks before the frost-free date for your area. Prepare a flat or bulb pan with a suitable germinating mixture—or use pre-moistened milled sphagnum moss—and sow seeds sparsely, covering to a depth of ⅛ inch. Seeds germinate best at 70° to 78° F., the higher temperature is recommended for hybrid sorts. When seedlings have expanded their seed-leaves—two or three days after germination begins—move to a very bright window or close under fluorescent lights, and hold at 68° to 72° F. Unless your germinating medium is well balanced and fortified, begin watering with a half-strength solution of balanced plant fertilizer when the first true leaves are 1 inch long. Repeat weekly. Strong seedlings come only with very strong light, ample fertilizer, a moderate temperature, and continuous moisture.

To start seeds in the garden, prepare the soil, set the tomato stakes, and at the base of each scrape a shallow, saucer-sized depression ¼ inch deep. Sow three seeds and cover with not more than ¼ inch of soil or germinating medium; sprinkle to moisten but avoid puddling the soil. Seedlings usually appear in four or five days in warm soil; when true leaves appear, push with a liquid fertilizer solution and thin to a single plant per stake. Because their roots never are disturbed, plants from direct-sown seed are surprisingly disease-resistant and often such plants bear as quickly as six-week-old transplanted plants set in the same day as seed is sown.

Tomato plants form roots the length of their stems. As tomatoes often suffer from lack of water during mid-summer, deep roots are very desirable. When you move tomato plants to the garden, at each stake dig a hole a foot or so deep; partially fill it with a rich mixture of compost or old manure and soil, and set the plant so only the terminal tuft of leaves is above ground level (you may have to remove several of the plant's lowest leaves). Partially fill the hole, and over subsequent days gradually pull in the soil. The deeply set plant will form roots along its buried length to build a very strong plant.

Space tomato plants according to their growth habit, your method of pruning, and your preference. Non-staked (determinate) tomatoes usually go 3 feet apart in the row with rows 4 feet apart. Even so, in humus and fertilizer-rich soil, plants will form a solid tangle before the last fruit ripens. By all means, when your non-staked tomato plants begin to branch and sprawl, mulch the earth in the tomato garden with 4 to 6 inches of loose, clean straw or hay. This holds moisture, reduces decay from mud-splash, and provides extra aeration to keep down leaf diseases.

Hybrid and indeterminate tomato plants ought to be severely pruned weekly for the biggest, best-developed fruits. Accordingly, the plants are narrow and can be planted more closely, as close as 2 feet apart in the row with rows 3 feet apart. However, where mechanical aids are used in the garden (power tillers, sprayers, and so on) slightly wider spacing is better. I recommend setting plants on 30-inch centers with rows on 42-inch centers. Even so, my Rototiller® is crowded out by mid-summer (at which time I quit tilling and put down straw).

Tomato soil needs to be slightly damp at all times; if allowed to dry out before watering begins, tomato fruit invariably develops blossom-end rot. The same disease, a physiological disorder, comes about with extreme heat, sharp differentials in temperature, or other environmental fluctuations. Likewise, the soil fertility needs to be kept reasonably constant. Organic fertilizers, spaded in during the fall, release nutrients into the soil gradually. It is a good idea to cultivate in dry commercial tomato fertilizer every three weeks or so, or water with a solution of soluble tomato fertilizer at two- to three-week intervals. Do not push plants with nitrogen-rich fertilizers as the succulent leaves will fall prey to various hard-to-control diseases, especially early blight or late blight. Shallowly hoe or otherwise till the tomato bed two or three times each week to maintain a dust mulch until straw is put down, or continue clean cultivation throughout the season.

When watering, use a canvas soil soaker or other basal irrigation device that does not wet the foliage. If you must apply overhead water, do so in early morning so mid-morning sun will dry the foliage.

Prune tomato plants each week. Suckers that get away and turn into flowering branches are difficult to remove. Tomato plants make branches at the base of every leaf. Flower clusters, however, appear directly from the stem and not at the leaf-bases.

The most severe pruning, as carried out by many truck gardeners and some home gardeners, consists of pinching out all branches (suckers) as they appear in the leaf axils. No branches at all are allowed to form. The bearing plant consists of a single upright (staked) stem with leaves and clusters of tomatoes along its length. A slight modification of this consists of removing all suckers entirely except the one directly below a cluster of fruit, and this sucker is allowed to make one leaf with the remainder pinched out. The idea is to increase the amount of foliage because the leaves manufacture food which is stored in the fruits. In very hot, sunny, climates, this sometimes is reversed, with the extra foliage allowed to develop directly above each fruit cluster so the extra leaves shade the tomatoes, preventing sunscald.

Another pruning method is to keep the primary stem free of all shoots, but the lowest sucker above ground is allowed to make a secondary shoot which also is kept free of suckers. Now you have a single stem up to the first leaf, then a main stem and a paralleling secondary stem, both free of suckers, but bearing leaves and fruit. Again, the modification of a partially pinched sucker just below (or above) each fruit cluster may be practiced.

It is best to prune back to not more than two branches per plant on indeterminate tomatoes, otherwise you will have an unwieldy bush that produces lots of foliage and a minimal amount of smallish tomatoes. Even with careful pinching and tying, modern tomato cultivars frustrate the most meticulous gardener. Suckers appear from below ground and you have to scrape away soil and cut them out. You pinch out a sucker (they should be pinched back when less than 3 inches long) from the axil of a leaf and a week or two later another has replaced it and has to be removed. Some European strains are especially prolific in making branching and leaf-bearing flower shoots. A normal flower spray appears and a few blooms open while the flower shoot grows longer and longer. Soon it branches and a few leaves appear here and there. The end result may be a massive cluster of thirty to fifty lemon-sized tomatoes of very mediocre quality. If a flower cluster continues to elongate, count out from the base five to ten blooms that have definitely set fruit, then nip it off.

It is impossible to over-stress the importance of pinching and tying tomato plants at least once each week. Skip a few extra days and your plants are uncontrolled bushes. Choose a training method and stick to it. If you are not sure which method is best for your strain of tomato, try a few plants different ways. Some cultivars respond better to single shoots than double, others make more and better-sized tomatoes with two trunks; the same applies to additional foliage from partially pinched suckers. You have to work out the best pruning method for your situation.

One thing is sure; clean wooden or metal stakes set firmly into the ground give best results. Every year new types of tomato supports appear on the market guaranteed to do away with pruning and tying. Their main function is to enrich the manufacturer and the retailer, while the gardener gets far fewer tomatoes. Buy or make sturdy stakes 6 to 8 feet long—18 inches to 2 feet goes into the soil, depending on soil texture—and set them in before setting plants. This is quickest and easiest, and a stake set before the plant goes into the ground will not sever any delicate roots.

Pests and Diseases

Tomatoes grown in a clean garden with no weeds around suffer from few insect pests. An occasional tobacco (tomato) hornworm will appear to quickly strip an entire plant of foliage and small fruits, but the daily gardener spots these as soon as a few leaves are chewed and dispatches the culprit under his heel. Later in the season corn earworms sometimes bore into tomatoes. If you are plagued with corn earworms, do a better job of grinding and composting all stalks—particularly cornstalks—as quickly as a crop is finished, and apply borer controlling chemicals to corn, squash, nearby dahlias, and other cane borer-susceptible species. Fall tilling becomes important when borers and earworms (tomato fruitworms) are a problem. Aphids sometimes appear and a quick dusting with diazinon or a nicotine compound controls these. If white fly begin to build up, spray the leaves from the undersides with malathion or another white fly controlling chemical at five-day intervals. Stick with it until the patch is free of white fly for two weeks. You may have to clean up nearby ornamental plantings, too. Nematodes sometimes parasitize tomato plant roots. There is nothing much you can do about these except chemically treat your soil; take up this operation with your County Extension Agent.

Tomato diseases, unfortunately, are common and widespread. In our favor, however, are disease-resistant strains. It pays to know which diseases are potential problems in your immediate area, and choose strains that resist or tolerate these. Such lists are published by your State University and are found at the County Extension Agent's office. Some common diseases are:

Vascular wilts; these are fungus diseases of the internal tissues of the plants. The parasitic fungi occur in the soil; the fungus moves into injured rootlets and begins to grow in the water-conducting tissues. Damage occurs in two ways: the fungus mass blocks water movements in the tomato tissues and at the same time the fungus secretes a toxic substance which diffuses to the upper parts of the plant causing a yellowing of the foliage and subsequent wilting before the fungus has reached that far. Nothing can be done to cure a plant affected with either of the wilt fungi known as fusarium and verticillium—hence, fusarium wilt and verticillium wilt. The disease-causing wilt fungi persist in the soil once infection occurs. The solution in this case is to plant wilt-resistant strains.

Several fungus diseases infect tomato leaves causing various wilts, leaf spots, or blotches. Full sun, good air circulation and water drainage, and careful attention to proper fertilizing reduces the danger of foliar diseases. Still, in a humid or rainy year, infection can occur. Some of the fungi spread rapidly and can destroy an entire planting in a short time. With the first sign of disease, spray or dust immediately with a tomato fungicide. As tomato plants respond badly to some fungicides, it is best to apply only those labeled as specific for tomato application.

Blossom-end rot occurs with alternately wet and dry soil, excessive summer heat, or other environmental abnormalities. The disease is said to be physiological. It begins with a shallow, blackish lesion on the tomato skin at the "bottom" where the blossom once was attached. The lesion grows, an irregular circle, gradually destroying the fruit. No amount of spraying cures this; keep soil uniformly moist during dry periods, mulch to reduce soil temperature, and avoid deep cultivation which disrupts roots.

Viruses of many sorts infect tomatoes; symptoms include mottling of leaves, crumpling of the foliage, elongation of internodes, and less definable indications. Some plants are hosts (reservoirs) to viruses and should be eliminated from the garden, or kept at some distance from the vegetable patch; these include pokeweed, petunias, tobacco and flowering tobacco. Potatoes also may be infected with viruses transmissible to tomatoes, but generally commercial potato strains are clean of viruses. (It is interesting to note that researchers of virus problems cannot be smokers because tobacco usually is virus-ridden and these viruses may be transmitted by touch.)

It is a good plan to keep tomato plants in the same part of the garden, and the soil very well reworked year after year, for five years or more. Invariably, soil-borne diseases build up, but by keeping the crop localized for a reasonable period, the disease is localized; then a shift can be made for several years to another portion of the garden, and so the entire garden does not become totally infected as it would be if the plants were annually shot-gunned hither and yon.

Occasionally tomato plants go bad for no apparent reason; when shoots elongate and go scrawny, leaves are abnormal, stunted, twisted and curled, often dark green, the problem is a hormone-type weed-killing chemical in the air. Somebody has used 2,4-D, 2,4,5 TP (silvex), or 2,4,5-T (brushkiller) and the fumes have carried (possibly for hundreds of yards) to damage or destroy the tomato plants. One of the strangest abnormalities of the tomato plant involves the walnut tree. Walnut leaves, roots, wood, and hulls contain a chemical, juglanin, which is very toxic to tomato plants. Mulch tomatoes with compost that includes walnut leaves and the tomatoes wilt and may die. Plant tomatoes in soil where walnut roots occur—or where an old walnut stump is decaying, and the plants wilt and die. Walnuts and tomatoes are incompatible.

Cultivars

Dozens of very good tomato strains are available to us today. They can be grouped in various ways: by growth habit— determinate, indeterminate, or as some of the newest ones, semi-determinate; by fruit form—globe, plum, pear, cherry, currant; by color—red, pink, orange, yellow, or white; by maturation—early, mid-season, and late; or by use—table, canning, paste, and as of late, container growing.

It should not be difficult to select the best strain of tomato for your garden. It should be a cultivar that is known to do well under local weather and soil conditions. It should suit your needs either as an all-purpose strain, or to supply tomatoes for canning, preserves, or another special use. If you make your own tomato paste you should plant **Roma, San Marzano,** or one of the other nearly juiceless, meaty, dark-red strains. Preserves usually are made from the plum- or pear-shaped fruits, either red or yellow. Cherry or currant tomatoes are handy for salads. My preference is for a few plants of an early strain to provide tomatoes in late June or early July, with the main crop of moderate-sized fruit suitable both for canning and for table use. As I grow in the same soil year after year, I plant only fusarium-, verticillium-, and nematode-resistant strains. The apartment, condominium, or town house gardener surely will want to grow a few of the newest dwarf plants that bear reasonable-sized fruits in pots.

Early Cultivars

Early Bird, 57 days; 5½-ounce fruit, globe-shaped. Indeterminate.

Early Fireball, 54 days; 3¼-ounce fruit, flat globe-shape. Indeterminate.

Early Summer Sunrise, 60 days; 5-ounce flat globe-shaped fruit. Indeterminate.

Gardener VF, 63 days; 6-ounce globe-shaped fruit. Indeterminate. Resists verticillium and fusarium wilt fungi.

Jetfire VF, 60 days; 7-ounce globe-shaped fruit. Determinate. Resists verticillium and fusarium wilt fungi.

Rushmore VF, 66 days; 7-ounce flat globe fruit. Indeterminate. Resists verticillium and fusarium wilt fungi.

Springset VF, 62 days; 6½-ounce deep globe fruit. Determinate. Resists verticillium and fusarium wilt fungi.

Starshot, 55 days; 3-ounce globe fruit. Indeterminate. Earliest verticillium wilt-tolerant strain.

Swift, 54 days; 2 ¾-ounce deep globe-shaped fruit. Indeterminate.

Ultra Girl VFN, 56 days; 7– 9-ounce globe. Semi-determinate (stake). Resists verticillium, fusarium wilt, and nematodes.

Main Crop Cultivars

Better Boy VFN, 72 days; to 16 ounces, deep globe. Indeterminate. Resists verticillium, fusarium wilt fungi, and nematodes.

Big Boy, 78 days; to 16 ounces, deep globe. Indeterminate.

Big Girl VF, 78 days; to 16 ounces, shallow globe. Indeterminate. Resists verticillium and fusarium wilt fungi.

Glamour, 74 days; 8–10 ounces, shallow globe. Indeterminate.

Jet Star, 72 days; 8-ounce globe. Indeterminate.

Moreton Hybrid, 70 days; 8 ounces, shallow globe. Indeterminate.

Ramapo, 85 days; 8–10 ounces, deep globe. Indeterminate. Resists verticillium and fusarium wilt fungi.

Rutgers 39 (VF), 80 days; 6–8 ounces, flattened globe. Indeterminate. Resists verticillium and fusarium wilt fungi.

Supersonic, 79 days; 6–10 ounces, shallow globe. Indeterminate. Resists verticillium and fusarium wilt fungi.

Pink-Fruited Cultivars

Oxhart, 86 days; 16 ounces, very deep globe. Indeterminate.

Ponderosa, 83 days; to 32 ounces, flattened, rough. Purplish-pink. Indeterminate.

Yellow-Fruited Cultivars (Large)

Jubilee, 72 days; 6-ounce globe. Indeterminate.

Sunray, 83 days; 8-ounce flattened globe. Indeterminate; yellow-orange. Resists fusarium wilt fungus.

Paste Tomatoes

Roma VF, 76 days; 4– 6-ounce cylindrical fruit. Determinate. Resists verticillium and fusarium wilt fungi.

San Marzano, 80 days; 4-ounce tapered cylindrical fruit.

Small Stature Plants for Pots or Boxes

Patio F, 70 days; 3– 5-ounce globe, 24-inch plant. Determinate. Resists fusarium wilt fungus.

Pixie, 52 days; 2– 3-ounce globe-shaped fruit; plant 14 to 18 inches tall. Determinate.

Small Fry VFN, 65 days; ¾-ounce globe. Plant to 30 inches. Determinate. Resists verticillium, fusarium wilt fungi, nematodes.

Tiny Tim, 55 days; ½ to ¾-ounce fruit, globe-shaped; plant to 15 inches. Determinate.

Old Standbys

For special purposes people still grow **Red Plum, Yellow Plum, Red Pear,** and **Yellow Pear** and, though disease-susceptible, they fill the need for preserving tomatoes. Other old-timers, good tomatoes all, such as **Bonny Best, Marglobe, Valient,** and the many canning strains released by Heinz and Campbell, should be avoided because of disease susceptibility. Modern disease-resistant strains of canning cultivars bred by the soup companies are available from truck garden seed specialists.

Turnip

Brassica rapa   Mustard Family

Turnips are cool-weather plants, though some of the newer hybrids tolerate more summer heat. In fact, there is no point in growing the older cultivars as the newest ones are far more tender and palatable. In my estimation there is little point in growing turnips at all as I do not care for the taste, and the turnip root, ninety percent water, with little sugar and no starch but containing pectase, a jelly-like carbohydrate, is not at all nutritious. The tops, rather like coarse spinach, are a better bet than the root for food, as they contain a high level of vitamin C and an appreciable amount of iron. The Japanese have taught us to pickle certain of the smaller turnip roots: Dice the roots, soak for one hour in salt water (⅔ cup water, 1 tablespoonful of salt), drain, and soak in pickling solution (⅔ cup vinegar, 5 tablespoonfuls sugar) overnight or longer. These make unusual hors d'oeuvres.

Soil Preparation

Turnip soil needs to be deeply turned, well furnished with organic residues applied to a previous crop; before planting, dress with 4 ounces per square yard of 5–10–5 fertilizer and fork twice. Where spring is long and drawn out, sow an early crop as soon as soil is workable; where summer is cool and rainy, try the new hybrids sown in April or May; anywhere, sow the main crop in August or September for a fall crop. In every case, work your soil very deeply and add inorganic fertilizer, very thoroughly incorporated, before planting.

Planting

Mark out drills one foot apart and open them to an inch or so deep. (Turnips make a fair cold frame crop, in which case, space rows on 6-inch centers.) For roots, sow seed two or three to an inch and thin when 3 or 4 inches high to stand 3 inches apart; thin later when roots are eating size to stand 6 to 9 inches apart, depending on mature size; for exhibition turnips, thin to 12 inches apart. For turnip greens, sow as above, but do not thin. Cover seed ⅓ to ½ inch deep. Seed germinates in five to ten days, depending on the strain.

Cultivation and Management

Flea beetles will devour your young turnips, beginning when tiny tops emerge from the soil. Begin spraying with diazinon, Sevin, or dust with rotenone as quickly as injury is noticed. Keep turnips in clean cultivation, breaking up the crust on the soil after each rainfall or watering. Like radishes, turnips are a fast-maturing crop, so little management is required if proper soil preparation is carried out before the seed is sown. But they must be kept clean and in loose soil. If root worms are a problem, check with your County Extension Agent for soil sterilization recommendations.

Cultivars

All Seasons, 28 days; globe-shaped, white, somewhat tolerant of hot and dry weather. Relatively new, a good turnip.

Extra Early White Ball, 25–30 days; a white, globe-shaped root with strap leaves; standard commercial sort.

Just Right, 35–40 days; an F_1 hybrid, flattened globe shape, pure white, both roots and tops said to be succulent and good, but strictly a fall crop as it goes to seed early if spring-sown.

Presto, 28 days; a small white Japanese turnip especially recommended for pickling.

Purple Top White Globe, 58 days; this is the standard, commercial turnip, rather flattened globe shape, white below, purple above, flesh crisp, both roots and tops edible.

Tokyo Market, 50 days; smooth, flattened white roots, flesh crisp and quite mild. Sow in early spring or fall as it is slow to bolt.

Watercress

Nasturtium officinale   Mustard Family

Widely naturalized in American streams, this cold water perennial should not be confused with the garden nasturtium *(Tropaeolum)*. To grow permanently, watercress requires cold, clean water; it grows floating and along the bank. Gardeners can grow watercress in the fall and early winter in a moist, shady garden bed, or the seedlings may be used as recommended for garden cress.

Soil Preparation

As the planting will not be permanent, fork up any well-manured, fertile soil in a shady part of the garden and broadcast pre-soaked seed or set in sprouted seedlings.

Planting

Soak cress seed for twenty-four hours in cool water; sow broadcast, two or three seeds to the square inch. Cover with ¼ inch of soil, then cover with clean burlap, kept damp, until germination begins. Remove burlap. Or sprout seedlings on wet paper towels.

Cultivation and Management

The cress crop will supply edible leafy shoot-tips in about fifty days; keep the planting quite damp, free of weeds. Clip 6-inch-high leafy shoots back halfway as often as they regrow. The cress bed may be covered with loose straw to carry it further into late fall, but when a heavy freeze knocks down the plants, spade them under to prevent overwintering insects and disease organisms.

If you have a cool stream or spring, pat cress seeds into the muddy rim just at the waterline and let nature take its course. Probably you will be supplied with watercress during cool weather forever after.

Watermelon

(See MELONS: Watermelon, page 109.)

Fertilizers for vegetables

Fertilizers supply essential minerals to plants, minerals needed to make protoplasm, and minerals needed to make the plants' various enzyme systems function properly. Nitrogen, a gas which makes up almost eighty percent of our atmosphere, is used by plants in a mineral form. It is converted by the plant to amino acids and these make up the protein of the plant. Phosphorus is an earth chemical and plants use in in the oxidized form. Within plant tissues phosphorus is essential to the transfer of energy which makes life possible. Potash is the "garden" name for potassium (the Greek word for it is Kalium so its chemical symbol is K), which also occurs in earth chemicals. Plants use substantial quantities of it in fruit and seed production. These three chemicals, nitrogen (N), phosphorus (P), and potassium (K), are used by plants in substantial quantities; they are known as the major plant nutritive elements. The chemicals supplying these essential nutrients may be soluble or relatively or completely insoluble. They may be mineral in form (as potassium nitrate, which supplies both potash and nitrogen) or organic as in a urea-form product. You will see numbers such as 5–10–5 or 10–10–10 on a fertilizer package or bag. This indicates five percent nitrogen as nitrate, ten percent phosphorus as phosphoric acid, and five percent potassium as potassium oxide, or ten percent each of nitrate nitrogen, phosphoric acid phosphorus, and potassium oxide potash.

Other minerals are needed by plants in extremely small quantities. These so-called trace elements are essential to healthy plant development. If they are lacking, plants fail to grow properly or they may not grow at all, or if they grow they may fail to set fruit. On the other hand, if the trace elements are present in excess the soil may be poisoned. Here is a case where a small amount of information is dangerous. People are coming to know the importance of trace elements so they look for fertilizers that contain them. Manufacturers are anxious to add trace elements to their fertilizers because one or two cents' worth per bag is more than ample to inflate the price of the fertilizer. If you suspect your soil is deficient in trace elements by all means have a capable technician run a series of tests. This is possible either through your County Extension Agent or a private soil-testing

172

laboratory. In any case, if you add trace elements to your soil once every ten years, in many cases once in a lifetime, that is sufficient. Do not buy fertilizer with trace elements every year. If you add too much of these, your soil will be poisonous to your plants and they will fail to grow properly. Some of the more common trace elements include boron, copper, magnesium, manganese, and zinc. In fertilizers they occur as oxides or in other salt forms.

Iron is an important chemical to plants as it is involved in chlorophyll production. Most soils contain a reasonable amount of iron, but sometimes it is not available to plants. If soil is too acidic or too alkaline the iron is "bound," unavailable for plant use. It is a good idea to have your soil tested for acidity frequently, and modify it so it is just to the acid side of the neutral point. Plants generally grow well in slightly acidic soil and iron is readily available to plants under these conditions. If your soil is known to be deficient in iron, add iron sulfate (sold in fertilizer shops as copperas, confusing as this is not a copper-containing product) to your compost or dress it over the soil at the rate of ¼ ounce per square yard. In some soils iron metabolism fails to function properly even when iron is present in substantial quantities. In such cases use one of the chelated iron preparations such as Sequestrene or Fe-Tracin. These contain iron in a form that is unaffected by abnormal soil conditions, so the iron will go into plant roots regardless of soil chemistry. When a plant is iron-deficient usually the leaves take on a yellow tinge or, in extreme cases, may go lemon-yellow. This condition is called chlorosis. When plants are chlorotic they need iron, and they need it fast. An iron chelate, applied to the soil and watered in, usually greens up a chlorotic plant in a day or two.

Calcium is used by plants in large quantities as it is the hardening agent for developing cell walls. Calcium also is involved in certain enzymatic activities. Gardeners supply calcium to their plants by adding some form of lime to the soil. Lime is powdered limestone, which commonly is calcium carbonate. Calcium carbonate is a tricky chemical to use as it affects the soil profoundly. Being extremely alkaline in reaction, it changes the soil pH (acidity level) markedly. It also affects the behavior of clay particles in the soil. You must remember certain basic practices when using lime in the garden. First, avoid the use of builder's lime (slaked or plasterer's lime) as its finely powdered condition is damaging to soil in almost every case. Rather, buy agricultural limestone which is ground to a gritty condition and dissolves gradually in the soil, working beneficially for soil *and* plants. Second, apply lime to spaded or plowed soil in the fall or very early spring; make a surface application as recommended by a soil-testing service and let the rain and weather carry it down through the soil particles. Later, fork it or till it throughout the soil. Third, *never* apply lime in any form as you add plant fertilizers or manure. There will be a destructive chemical reaction if you do. You can prove this to yourself by holding a bit of 5–10–5 fertilizer in your hand; stir in a pinch of powdered lime with your finger, then sniff. That pungent aroma is your nitrogen going off as ammonia gas. Applications of fertilizers and lime (in any form) should be separated by three to five weeks.

When available, always buy dolomitic limestone for your garden. This is a calcium-magnesium carbonate which automatically supplies essential magnesium to the soil in the best possible (relatively insoluble) form. As you travel across the country you can tell where farmers use dolomitic limestone in many cases because pastures and cereal crops are exceptionally dark green and lush. It is a fine chemical.

Lime is also available from bonemeal. Old-time garden "experts" discourage the use of bonemeal and like to point out that a buried bone takes decades to decay in the soil (so long as it is undecayed the lime in the bone is unavailable to plants). But they are not considering two factors. First, powdered bone, which is bonemeal, is quickly attacked by soil organisms and reduced to a soluble state. In healthy, high-humus soil powdered bone is converted to soluble lime solution within a few weeks. Second, bonemeal has changed these days. The U.S. Government, fearing the transmission of one or two rare diseases from dead cattle, requires that all bonemeal in the U.S. be steamed to sterilize it, and steaming markedly modifies the solubility of bonemeal. Steamed bonemeal is many, many times more soluble than raw bonemeal, which no longer is marketed. So pay no attention to these people who say that bonemeal is too slow-acting. If your soil is at all supplied with humus and moisture, modern steamed bonemeal will break down relatively quickly, releasing calcium and other chemicals. In composts it functions at about the same rate as coarse agricultural limestone.

Leafy vegetables need quite a lot of fertilizer, especially nitrate fertilizer. Fruiting vegetables need only a modest amount of nitrogen but they need phosphates and potash. Root vegetables and tubers need moderate amounts of all three major elements, but it is important for the chemicals to be distributed very thoroughly through the soil rather than in streaks which result from incomplete tillage. Modern fertilizers are fairly soluble. When the product is scattered over the soil and tilled in (*never leave fertilizer exposed to air*) it takes up moisture from the soil and begins to "melt." Once in solution, it can be washed downward by rainwater or irrigation water, eventually going beyond the reach of plant roots. For this reason, we usually dress fertilizer on the soil as we work it up for a crop. We fork it in, open our drills, sow seed, and when the seeds germinate, the fertilizer is there to be used. It is best to make a modest application of fertilizer at the time of seedbed preparation, and then side-dress the crop with fertilizer, dribbling small amounts along both sides of the row of plants (hoe it in) two or three times through the development of the crop. This gives a steady supply of fertilizer and is most effective.

For very small gardens and for plants grown in containers there is an easier way. Apply liquid fertilizer to your plants at biweekly intervals. For leafy crops, use the home-prepared solution full strength as recommended by the manufacturer, for fruit (beans, tomatoes, squash) and root (beet, radish, carrot) crops dilute it by half. Even in my big garden I resort to liquid fertilizer from time to time because it gives plants a quick boost. I like to apply it in fine droplets from a sprinkling can directly over the leaves and soil, because some will be absorbed directly by the foliage. Early morning is a good time to do this because the foliage will be dry before strong sunlight has a chance to do damage.

One of my favorite fertilizers is *liquid* manure (something quite different from dried manure or dried manure–compost combinations). This is a very old-fashioned way of growing plants, but it gives outstanding results. And it is as easy for the penthouse gardener as it is for the country man. You need either a purchased bag of dehydrated cow manure or some chips fresh from the pasture—fresh enough that they have not laid out through a rain. Fill a muslin bag with this crumbled manure and hang the bag in a container of water. In the old days we used a 10- or 25-pound muslin sugar sack and hung it in the rain barrel. Today it is easier to stitch up a bag that is flat, 6 to 10 inches wide and 12 to 18 inches long. It will hang, tied with twine, in a 30-gallon plastic trash container very nicely. The resulting dark tea-colored liquid is filled with minerals needed by the plants and with humic acids which do wonders for both soil and roots. If you have never used manure water on your plants, give it a try this year. You will be astonished at the results.

Composts and manures for vegetables

Composts are made of decayed vegetable matter; if the compost heap contains a mixture of garden debris we simply call the finished product "compost." If we have carefully piled only leaves the result is "leaf mold" or, perhaps, "oak leaf mold." Sometimes we are able to stack up sod (always pile it grass-side downward) and the resulting product is "fibrous loam."

Manures most commonly are animal manures. It may be horse manure from the stable, in which case quite a lot of straw is included. It may be dairy cow manure, which is nearly pure animal waste, or it may be from a feed lot which is straw and cow manure. Rarely do we use poultry manure, pigeon manure, or rabbit manure, and even less frequently does someone have access to manure from the pigsty. Horses and cows feed largely on hay or grass and thus their manures are remarkably similar to carefully made garden compost because the raw ingredients are similar. Cow manure, due to the cow's four-stage digestive system, is rather thoroughly digested. It will not make a hot compost if stacked. Horse manure, only partially digested, will begin to ferment with considerable production of heat when stacked (I have known stable manure piles to catch fire from their own heat). So horse manure must be stacked for a brief period, then the pile broken down and restacked to keep high temperatures from damaging the product. Other manures must be layered with garden debris from the compost pile; they are very difficult to use "as is."

There is a great misunderstanding about the value of dry animal manures and composts in gardening. Some gardeners attempt to equate these products with fertilizers. There is little similarity. Fertilizers supply minerals to the soil, minerals needed by the plants for growth processes. Manures and composts supply humus-yielding products to the soil. They contribute the essential organic fraction which makes soil workable, amenable to healthy root growth, well-aerated, and at the same time moisture-retentive.

I would not try to garden without composts, manures, and

other sources of organic residues such as mulches of sawdust and straw. But I certainly would not rely on these soil-texturizing agents for mineral nutrition for my plants. A *ton* of fresh barnyard manure that never has been leached by rain contains about as much nitrate, phosphate and potash as an 80-pound bag of 5–10–5 fertilizer! Manure that has been exposed to weather and to rain is almost free of available minerals. That is not to say it is not of value in the garden. It is of great value as a source of organic residues which do so much to texture the soil and make it good for plant roots.

The point is, we use composts and manures as soil-texturing agents. We use fertilizers as sources of minerals which make our plants grow vigorously. The wise gardener uses all the organic residues he can lay his hands on, and he adds fertilizers in conjunction with his manures and composts.

In the vegetable garden we dress the soil with manure and compost in the fall and spade these organics in as deeply as possible. If our soil is shallow, we double-dig or trench. In the early spring we lime the soil if a test indicates that lime is needed, and as we fork up sections of the plot to prepare seedbeds, we add fertilizers. More finished (crumbly brown) compost or well-rotted manure is used through the summer; we mulch the space between our rows with it as the summer turns hot and dry. This material helps hold soil moisture and it acts as an insulating agent, giving our plants a cooler root run. In my Midwestern garden I find it necessary to use quantities of straw in mid-summer. Hot-weather crops such as corn and squash usually take the sun-baked soil, but other crops respond well to 6 inches or more of loose straw tossed on top of manured or compost-dressed soil that has been thoroughly cultivated. When I put down straw I scatter a very light dressing (not more than half an ounce per square yard) of ammonium nitrate over the mulch. If I use sawdust for the mulch—which I do for melons, canteloupes and the like because squash bugs hide too well in the straw—I dissolve a high nitrate fertilizer in water and sprinkle the sawdust generously with the solution.

At the end of the season, spade your summer mulches into the soil with added manure and compost. As crops finish up, pull the plants and compost them. Because vegetable plants may be infested with insect parasite eggs or disease spores, it is a good idea to either shred the material before composting or else add sufficient manure and fertilizer to the compost pile so it heats up, growing hot enough to destroy pests and diseases. Whenever I have time, I run my compost (finished) through a shredder to mix it, and then restack it for treatment with Dowfume, a sterilizing gas which is applied very carefully under a plastic sheet in the open garden.

Not all crops grow optimally on newly manured soil. Be sure to plan your planting schedule so plants are set where they will succeed best. Optimally, one-third or one-half of the garden should be very heavily manured each year, and those crops which thrive on freshly manured soil go on the manured portion, the others on the area which was manured the previous year. In the A to Z section on vegetables, mention is made, where applicable, of plants which grow best on freshly manured or on unmanured soil.

It is almost impossible to use too much manure or compost on vegetable garden soil so long as you do it the right way. Make your major applications in the fall. Add more, but only thoroughly decayed manure or compost, through summer. Your vegetable plot will increase in productivity every year. And you will have less trouble with certain plant diseases and parasites when the soil is rich in humus.

There is one more manure form to mention. Green manure. Green manure is plant material that is turned under while green and growing. If your garden plot is divided into separate beds you can use the green manure technique very well. Otherwise, you have to do only a part of the garden at a time so green manuring does not interfere with planting.

When a lush, dense stand of plants is spaded under (it is essential that the plants be buried completely), these quickly decay in place and the result is a localized compost of a fibrous nature, excellent for loosening a tight, compacting soil. Here are some green manuring methods:

In late summer, clear one bed or a portion of the garden, then till the soil adding a balanced fertilizer such as 5–10–5 at the rate of about 4 ounces per square yard. Rough-rake the area and dress with rye, winter wheat, or barley seed, ½ to ¾ pound per 100 square feet, and rake again to lightly cover the seed. Walk down or roll. Four to six weeks before the killing frost date is a good time to plant your green manure crop. The cereal will germinate and make good plants in the fall and will stool out in early spring. Before it is more than 12 inches high, spade it under, then dress the rough-turned soil with agricultural limestone if a test indicates it is needed. A month later the soil can be forked up for planting.

In mid-summer you can work up the soil and plant soybeans; these thrive on heat and will make sizable plants before frost. When frost is anticipated, spade them under (much value is lost if the leaves are frost-blackened), and if you wish, sow a cereal crop for winter green manuring.

Another way; any time through summer hoe up the soil between rows and sow thickly with oats. As these become high enough to interfere with the crops on each side, spade them in. Rape, collards, safflower, and some of the fast-growing legumes all make good cool or hot season green manure crops. Green manures are widely used almost everywhere outside the United States; we need to learn more about this excellent way to add humus to the soil.

Growing vegetables in containers

For the city gardener or gardener with very limited space, there are a few kinds of vegetables that can be grown successfully in containers. Generally speaking, these are vegetables where a single "piece" feeds two or three people. To produce well-formed, well-flavored vegetables on plants grown in containers you have to start with the correct soil mixture in the correct container and follow through with cultural practices that will bring the plants into strong, productive growth.

Vegetable plants are a result of decades, even centuries, of selective breeding. Breeding carried on in deep, rich soil in open fields. We have to bear these field conditions in mind when we attempt to get the same plants to produce in what amounts to confinement. The containers have to be generous in size, and have very good drainage. The soil must be very porous, well aerated, moderately fertile, and somewhat moisture-retentive. When we begin with the correct container and proper soil mix our chances of success are well based.

Select containers that suit the decor of your growing area. If this is the terrace of your cedar condominium, by all means consider the ready-made wooden tubs found in garden shops. If you are terrace or balcony gardening in the southwest or in Florida, think in terms of very large terra-cotta pots. Perhaps your vegetable garden is relegated to the service area of your balcony or roof garden—even to the fire escape (be sure that your containers do not obstruct free movement on a fire escape as this is a legal offense in many places). In such a case you may wish to grow vegetables in bushel baskets. Whatever the type of container selected, it needs to be a minimum of 12 inches deep, 12 to 18 inches wide, and sturdy enough to hold up for one season. Avoid a container that may give off toxic chemicals into the rooting mixture—some waterproof cartons and shipping containers fall into this category.

If you are engaged in balcony gardening you may have trouble with soil that is too hot because the sun hits the sides of your containers. Avoid those containers that rapidly transfer solar or ambient air heat to the soil—most metal containers and some plastics belong here. If you are not sure of the chemical or insulation potentials of your "found" container, be on the safe side and apply a generous layer of common roofing tar (NOT driveway asphalt) to the inside as this material is chemically neutral and the insulation effect is good. After such a sealing job, redrill the drainage holes in the container as probably the tar has blocked them. Another way to cope with this problem is to design planter boxes, fill these loosely with straw or other porous material, and plunge your planted pots in this strawy bed which will insulate them from outside heat. Still another solution is to line a large pot with wet sphagnum moss and slip your planted pot into this jacket. With containers you can use some of the lightweight, porous, inorganic mulches. These pebble-like materials look well, they prevent mud from splashing as you water, and they keep the soil from crusting.

There's little point in filling your container with the heavy soils of the garden. Usually these garden soils, when moved into containers, settle, compact, and lose porosity and aeration before one season is finished. If you do opt for garden soil, mix it with very generous amounts of coarse organic debris such as chopped straw, coarse compost, or coarse leaf mold. In any case, a 2- or 3-inch layer of fresh straw, peat chunks, or even pebbles in the bottom of each container helps insure good drainage.

Several soil mixtures are suitable for vegetable growing in containers. One of the easiest is the familiar:

1 part garden loam
1 part coarse brown peat
1 part coarse, clean sand

In this case, parts are by bulk (volume). The peat should be slightly damp when mixed in, and soil, peat, and sand should be free of very fine particles that clog drainage. To a bushel of this mix, add a heaping cupful of steamed bonemeal.

A lighter-weight mix that gives good results is:

1 peck measure of garden loam
2 dry quart measures of leaf mold
1 dry quart measure of brown peat
1 to 2 dry quart measures of perlite

For this mix, the peat and leaf mold should be slightly moist; adjust the volume of perlite to suit your cultural practices; if you use the larger amount you will have to fertilize more often. As perlite is a lightweight, inert product, it aids greatly in making up lightweight potting media. In any case, to a bushel of the finished mixture, add a generous cupful of steamed bonemeal and a tablespoonful of timed-release 5–10–5 fertilizer.

Temper the moisture content of your soil mix before filling your container. Never pour dry soil mix into a container and then water it in place as it puddles and aeration channels are clogged. The best watering method is to spread the finished mix in a 2-inch layer on a clean concrete floor or asphalt-paved driveway; sprinkle with water from a can with a fine rose ("head") until the surface of the soil is quite wet. Cover with paper and allow to rest overnight. Then turn the soil, mixing thoroughly, cover, and allow to rest again. When the soil mix is crumbly, with no trace of muddiness, pour it loosely into the container—tap the container as it is filling to somewhat settle the soil mix—and you are ready for plants or for seeds.

Now that we have the container filled with a recommended soil mix over a generous straw layer, what shall we grow in it?

Tomatoes are a good bet. In fact, you can grow the smaller-sized tomato plants such as *Tom Thumb* and *Patio* in a half-bushel basket or a 12-inch clay pot. But the full-sized varieties such as *Rutgers, Big Boy, Better Boy,* and *Supersonic* need a bushel-sized container—one plant per container, and by all means, stake that plant. To grow tomatoes most effectively, set a single plant in the center of the container, burying a good portion of the stem at planting time. I prefer to dig a hole deep enough to set the plant in right up to its first true leaf. As tomato plants make roots from stem tissue that is buried, such a deep-planted plant will develop an exceptionally strong root system early in life to help it along. Set your stake when you set your plant, and as the young plant grows, prune it according to instructions in a pruning book.

Your tomato plant cannot be set until danger of frost is past. At first it will grow rather slowly. There is a chance, if your weather is not too hot, that you can grow a temporary fringe of quick-maturing salad truck around the rim of the basket or box. This only works if the temperature is in the seventies or just somewhat lower. Three inches in from the rim of the container scratch a groove (lift out the soil, do not press it down) half an inch deep. In this little drill, sparsely sow 24 to 28 day radishes or an early maturing leaf lettuce such as *Salad Bowl, Black Seeded Simpson,* or *Oakleaf.* I never have had luck with *Ruby* or the other colored strains, and the heading lettuces take too long to mature. Whatever you grow—if anything—as a "catch" crop, it must be out of the container by the time the tomato plant begins to set fruit. Once your plant or plants are growing, proceed as you would in the open garden so far as culture is concerned. Only watering will vary. Your soil always should be barely moist, never dry, but never wet for any length of time.

The bush-type summer squashes sometimes make decent crops in large containers. Success seems to depend on shelter from wind; uniform soil moisture, rather damper than for tomatoes; and several plants to assure pollination of the female blossoms. Fill your box or basket as for the tomato plant—for any sort of squash a bushel of soil is necessary. Draw the soil into a shallow mound in the container and in the center, 3 inches apart each way, poke in, half an inch deep, four or five seeds of bush summer squash such as **Patty Pan** or **Yellow Crook Neck,** any of the several zucchinis, or the new hybrids of the Crook Necks which have straight necks and marvelous flavor. When the seedlings develop three or four true leaves, thin to three plants per bushel-sized container. Never allow your squash plants to wilt for lack of water. On hot, sunny days, you may need to water two or three times daily when the plants are fully grown and producing.

Bush green beans make moderately good container plants but the yield is not nearly so good per plant as open garden-grown bean plants. For these use a bushel basket or similarly sized container to hold five plants in a ring one-third of the way in from the rim, with a single plant in the center. Or grow them in 10-inch pots, one or two plants per pot. Another container way with beans is a window box at least 8 inches deep and wide, and as long as you wish. Either of the above soil mixtures will suffice. Sow the beans after danger of frost is past in a drill 1-inch deep; later thin to stand 8 inches apart in the row. Soil for beans should always be barely moist, never wet for a prolonged period, and full sun is essential. Do not handle bean plants when the foliage is damp as a rust disease will become a problem.

By all rights, it should be possible to grow top-quality peppers and eggplants in containers, but in my experience both do poorly. Apparently, they require a more constant soil temperature and moisture level than is possible in a container. But if you are more interested in the ornamental value of the plants than you are in the yield, try them, proceeding as for tomatoes. For both, stakes are important; a 24-inch stake usually suffices. Full sun, again, is critical.

There is little point in trying members of the cabbage family in a container. These demand cool, compact, damp soil, and it is almost impossible to meet these requirements in a container.

Quick-maturing leafy crops such as cress, spinach (only in cool weather), and the leaf lettuces develop moderately well in containers. But there is a catch. You go to no end of trouble to get the right container and to locate proper components for a proper soil mixture. You temper your soil, fill your container, sow your seed, and spend a few minutes (or more) every day for at least four weeks watering, cultivating, weeding, and generally tending the crop. Then it is ready to pick. And there goes your crop! It takes all the lettuce you can raise in two bushel baskets to make one bowl of wilted lettuce for three or four people. It takes all the spinach you can grow in 10 feet of window box to make a single meal for Mom, Dad, and two kids. You pick the crop and you are done. Of course, if you live in lonely splendor, you can harvest a few mature leaves from each plant for salads or sandwiches, leaving the plants to grow on, and stretch the yield. But it is a pretty unrewarding experience.

What about fertilizing vegetable crops in containers? That steamed bonemeal in the soil mix will yield nutrients over quite a long period. But it doesn't do any harm to add small amounts of water-soluble fertilizer to the water that goes on the soil every second or third week. If you are growing tomatoes, peppers, beans, or a similar "fruit" crop, use a fertilizer that is moderately low in nitrogen and higher in phosphate and potash, such as a 10–20–20 or a similar formula. Use this at half the strength recommended by the manufacturer. If you grow ornamentals using water-soluble fertilizer, for the "fruit" crops choose the fertilizer intended for flowering plants rather than for foliage plants. The foliage plant fertilizer, always high in nitrogen, is the right one for leaf crops such as lettuce, upland cress, and spinach. These can be pushed with a half-strength solution applied at weekly intervals. Always apply a fertilizer solution to soil that already is slightly damp, never quite dry. Such an application is better in the early morning than in the evening.

Almost no vegetables are adaptable for hanging basket culture. But there is an exception. If you can locate seed or plants of the currant tomato, *Lycopersicon pimpinellifolium,* set one plant in the center of a very heavily mossed basket (at least 12 inches in diameter, larger is better) filled with either of the recommended soil mixtures. Pinch the plant when it has six true leaves, hang it in a sunny, windless place, keep the soil evenly moist, never soggy, and watch it branch to a huge, cascading specimen, completely covered with clusters of tiny, delicious tomatoes!

Glossary

Aeration. A term applied to soils, referring to a loose condition which allows air to move through the topsoil. Spaded or forked soil usually is sufficiently aerated for most vegetables.

Annual. A plant that survives for only one season. Most vegetables grow as annuals but some live for more than one year, as do beets, cabbages, or artichokes.

Axil. The angle between the leaf stalk and stem in which a bud (which eventually becomes a shoot or flower) is found.

Bed. A garden area of prepared soil, with or without plants.

Biennial. A plant which makes leafy growth one year, overwinters, then makes flowers, fruits, and dies the second season.

Blanching. The technique of covering stems of certain plants with soil or other light-excluding materials to bleach out all chlorophyll and make the plant tissue tender; applies to celery, cardoons, and a few other species.

Bolting. A condition, usually due to hot or dry weather, when a leafy vegetable such as lettuce, chinese cabbage, radish, or true cabbage throws a seed stalk while foliage deteriorates.

Compost. Partially decomposed plant residues (sometimes mixed with animal manures) which are rich in fiber and humic acids. Composts greatly improve soil texture but add only small amounts of fertility.

Cover. To bury seeds after sowing to speed germination. Fine seeds usually are not covered; most seeds are covered about twice their height as they lie in the drill, a few are buried more deeply.

Crown. The uppermost part of a rootstock from which leaves and shoots break, for example, the crowns of rhubarb or asparagus.

Cultivar. A variety of plant which has been created under cultivation rather than occurring naturally.

Damping-off. A seedling disease caused by any of several fungi, in which recently emerged seedlings topple over, having been girdled by disease at the groundline. In cool weather, combat with terrachlor; in warm weather, with Dexon.

Drainage. The downward movement of water through soil as opposed to runoff, which refers to water sheeting over the surface of the soil.

Dress. Also, top-dress. To scatter fertilizer, manure, or compost over the soil surface. Fertilizers usually are then tilled into the soil; manures and composts are often left on top.

Drill. An open furrow in which seed is sown. Depth is adjusted to the individual crop.

Embryo. The rudimentary plant within a seed, which, during germination, produces first a root, then a shoot.

Eye. Usually the bud or bud area of a tuber, such as a potato.

Fertilizer. A product containing one or more chemical elements required for plant growth, such as nitrates, phosphates, or potash. A complete fertilizer contains all three of these major elements.

Frame. A structure, usually rectangular, which covers a bed and which in turn is covered with a glazed sash. Frames are used to create a controlled environment for seed germination or seedling cultivation. Without supplemental heat it is a cold frame; with supplemental (usually bottom) heat it is a hotbed.

Fungicide. A product that controls diseases caused by fungi. Most fungicides are protective in nature and must be on the plant to *prevent* infection as they do not eradicate fungi that have already penetrated plant tissues.

Germination. The first stage of growth when a seed takes on water and the embryo resumes growth, breaking through the seed coat.

Green Manure. Any leafy crop grown to be spaded under while in succulent growth. Green manures greatly improve soil texture.

Hardening-off. The technique of moving indoor-grown plants to a *sheltered* outdoor position for a few days while tissues firm up. The hardened plants then are transplanted to a fully exposed growing site.

Head. A short, dense spike of flowers (broccoli, cauliflower) or leaves (cabbage, lettuce).

Hill. (1) a mound of earth on which seed for plants requiring sharp drainage is sown, as melons or cucumbers; or (2) soil pulled toward a clump or row of growing plants to further bury roots, as for sweet corn or potatoes.

Humus. The residue of decayed organic matter; usually a brownish, amorphous mass, spongy in nature, which greatly enhances soil texture, moisture retention, and mineral holding capacities.

Insecticide. A substance that kills insects; usually applied as a spray or a dust. Apply any poison in the vegetable garden as a last resort and only use insecticides recommended for vegetables, carefully following the directions for proper application.

Intercrop. The practice of growing a quick-maturing crop between rows or plants of a slower maturing vegetable, such as radishes between peas or parsnips, lettuces between cabbages.

Internode. The portion of a stem between two joints or nodes.

Joint. *See* Node.

Leaching. The downward washing through the soil of nutrient elements by draining rainwater or irrigation water. Soluble fertilizers may be quickly lost from the upper layer of soil due to leaching.

Lift. To carefully dig up a plant, preserving the root system. Vertically insert a spade or fork well back from a plant that is to be lifted, then pry gently, working from all sides, until the plant can be raised with the roots intact.

Loam. Soil with balanced amounts of sand, silt, clay, and organic residues that supports vigorous plant growth and is easily worked.

Major Element. A chemical element, usually occurring in salt form, required by plants in substantial quantities. Major elements are nitrogen (as nitrates or ammonium or urea compounds), phosphates, and potassium (as potash). Also needed in substantial amounts are calcium (from limestone), iron, and magnesium, which occurs in chlorophyll.

Manure. Commonly, animal feces, especially cow or horse dung with or without bedding material. Fresh manures are applied only in fall or winter; well-rotted manures may be worked through soil any time. Bagged, dehydrated manures usually are fresh, too hot for direct application to growing plants.

Mineral. A chemical in the inorganic form,

that is, without carbon chains. Fertilizer salts and most spray products are in mineral form.

Molluscicide. A product, usually poisoned bait, that attracts and kills snails and slugs.

Mound. *See* Hill.

Mulch. Loose, porous material or a continuous filament laid on the surface of soil to retard weed growth, to retain moisture, and to cool the soil. Mulches may be organic, as chopped straw, coarse compost, or sawdust; or inorganic, such as rock chips, or film coverings such as aluminum foil or polyethylene.

Nematodes. Almost microscopic, soil-borne eelworms. They may be harmless or may be a plant-parasitizing specie that invades all parts of a plant causing a general deterioration of tissues. If nematodes are suspected, send fresh soil and plant samples to the County Extension Agent for analysis.

Node. The portion of a stem where one or more leaves and axillary buds occur.

Nutrient. A product utilized by plants for growth. *See* Fertilizer.

Open-Pollinated. Pollination taking place in a "natural" way, either wind or insects or plant movements transferring the pollen necessary to fertilize flowers.

Overlick. Refers usually to excessive rotary cultivation which overaerates soil while destroying soil structure. Overlicked soil at first is loose and fluffy, but crusts and bakes after a rain.

Peat. Organic (plant) matter in an arrested state of decay which is valuable in improving soil texture and moisture-retaining characteristics. Peat *always* should be thoroughly incorporated in soil, never left on the surface to dry.

Perennial. A plant that lives on for several seasons, such as artichokes or multiplier onions.

Pesticide. Any product intended to kill animals, including insects, which invade the garden. These include arachnicides (miticides), molluscicides, rodenticides.

Repellent. A product that discourages animals without harming them, usually by a noxious odor or by taste. Repellents are available for dogs, cats, rodents, and deer.

Slug. A destructive relative of the snail; con-trolled in the garden by poison bait usually containing metaldehyde which is a molluscicide.

Snail. A destructive mollusc; *See* Slug.

Sow. To lay seed on or in the soil. In the vegetable garden, seed usually is sown in drills to be covered to a depth appropriate for the species.

Spit. (1) A spade blade's depth in the soil, usually ten to 14 inches deep; (2) the "piece" of soil picked up by the spade blade when fully inserted into the soil.

Systemic. A prophylactic product which works from within a plant as an insecticide or (rarely) as an insecticide. Systemics may be sprayed on to be taken in through the leaves, or, more commonly, applied through the soil for root absorption. Systemics usually are *not* used in the vegetable garden or on food crops.

Tilling. Cultivating of soil by spading, forking, plowing, or by any other method.

Tilth. Crumbly soil structure provided by good tillage.

Trace Element. A nutrient element essential to normal plant growth but which must be present only in very small quantities. Trace elements include boron, copper, manganese, zinc, and some others known to be essential to only a few plants.

Transplant. (1) To dig up and reset, as with young cabbage and tomato plants; (2) as a noun, referring to the plant that has been moved.

Virus. A disease-causing agent much smaller than a bacterium; usually transmitted in the garden by aphids, leaf hoppers, and other insects with piercing-sucking (mosquito-like) mouthparts. There is no treatment for viruses in plants; normal control includes use of immune or resistant species, insect control, and destruction of mosaic-infected plants, particularly weeds known to harbor quantities of viruses, such as pokeweed.

Wood Ash. The product of burnt wood. If unleached it contains about seven per cent potash as potassium carbonate and may be applied to soil as potash fertilizer not exceeding eight ounces per square yard.

Quick Reference Chart

Vegetable	Seed Quantity	Days to Mature	Sow*	Harvest
Bean, broad	¼ lb. sows 50-ft. row	65 to 90	38° O. (early as possible)	late spring to early summer
Bean, green bush	¼ lb. sows 35-ft. row	40 to 58	58° O. to mid-summer	mid-summer to frost
Bean, lima	¼ lb. sows 40-ft. row	60 to 75	62° O. to mid-spring	late summer to frost
Bean, pole	¼ lb. sows 25 hills	55 to 65	58° O. to mid-summer	mid-summer to frost
Bean, soy	¼ lb. sows 40-ft. row	85 to 110	62° O. to mid-summer	late summer to frost
Beans, kidney, navy, hort.	¼ lb. sows 40-ft. row	100 to 110	55° O. to mid-summer	late summer to frost
Beet	¼ oz. sows 25-ft. row	34 to 75	45° O. to mid-summer; or early fall	early summer to frost
Broccoli	⅛ oz. yields 350 plants	70 to 98	I., 3 to 6 wks. before L.K.F. date	late spring to frost
Brussels sprouts	⅛ oz. yields 350 plants	95 to 138	I., 3 to 6 wks. before L.K.F. date	late summer to early winter
Cabbage, early	⅛ oz. yields 350 plants	62 to 70	I., 3 to 6 wks. before L.K.F. date	early summer to mid-summer
Cabbage, mid-season	⅛ oz. yields 350 plants	67 to 85	I., 3 to 6 wks. before L.K.F. date	mid-summer
Cabbage, late	⅛ oz. yields 350 plants	75 to 90	on or after L.K.F. date	late summer to frost
Cabbage, Savoy	⅛ oz. yields 350 plants	72 to 86	I., 3 to 6 wks. before L.K.F. date	mid-summer to frost
Chinese Cabbage	⅛ oz. yields 350 plants	60 to 80	According to strain	early summer to frost
Carrot	⅛ oz. sows 40-ft. row	55 to 70	I., 3 wks. before L.K.F. date	early summer to frost
Cauliflower	⅛ oz. yields 400 plants	48 to 70	I., 3 to 6 wks. before L.K.F. date	early summer (also late fall)
Celeriac	1/16 oz. yields 800 plants	110	65° O. to early summer	late summer to early winter
Celery	1/16 oz. yields 850 plants	90 to 110	65° O. to early summer	late summer to early winter
Collards	1/16 oz. sows 25-ft. row	70 to 85	Early spring or late summer	early summer or late fall
Corn, sweet	¼ lb. sows 150- to 200-ft. row	54 to 94	62° O. to late summer	early summer to frost
Cucumber, slicing	¼ oz. sows 25 hills	52 to 80	68° to mid-summer	mid-summer to frost
Cucumber, pickling	¼ oz. sows 25 hills	48 to 65	68° to mid-summer	mid-summer to frost
Eggplant	1/16 oz. yields 125 plants	56 to 85	75° to mid-summer (may start I.)	late summer to frost
Endive; escarole	¼ oz. sows 25-ft. row	85 to 100	50° to 65° O., spring or early fall	early summer or late fall
Kale	¼ oz. sows 50-ft. row	55 to 65	48° to 55° O., spring or late summer	early summer or fall
Kohlrabi	¼ oz. sows 50-ft. row	50 to 55	48° to 55° O., spring or late summer	early summer or fall
Leek	¼ oz. sows 50-ft. row	75 to 100	60° O. or start early I.	late summer through mild winter
Lettuce, head	⅛ oz. sows 40-ft. row	80 to 95	1 to 4 wks. before L.K.F. date	mid-summer
Lettuce, leaf	⅛ oz. sows 40-ft. row	45 to 70	1 to 5 wks. before L.K.F. date	late spring to early summer
Okra	½ oz. sows 25-ft. row	50 to 70	70° O. to early summer	mid-summer to early fall
Onions, bunch	¼ oz. sows 50-ft. row	60 to 70	60° O. to early summer, or start I.	mid-summer
Onions, to dry	¼ oz. sows 50-ft. row	90 to 110	70° I.; transplant after L.K.F. date	late summer to fall
Parsnip	⅛ oz. sows 25-ft. row	110 to 120	60° to mid-spring	fall to early winter
Peas	¼ lb. sows 30-ft. row	55 to 70	48° O. to mid-spring (where cool)	late spring to early summer
Pepper, sweet	⅛ oz. yields 250 plants	55 to 75	70° I.; transplant when quite warm	mid-summer to frost
Pepper, hot	⅛ oz. yields 250 plants	60 to 75	70° I.; transplant when quite warm	mid-summer to frost
Radish	⅛ oz. sows 25-ft. row	20 to 35	40° O. (spring); 60° O. (late summer)	spring and fall
Rutabaga	⅛ oz. sows 30-ft. row	95 to 100	55° O. to mid-spring	late summer to late fall
Salsify	¼ oz. sows 25-ft. row	115	60° O. to mid-spring	late summer to winter
Spinach	¼ oz. sows 25-ft. row	48 to 50	40° O. (spring); 55° O. (early fall)	late spring; late fall
Squash, summer	Varies with strain	40 to 70	65° O. to mid-summer	mid-summer to frost
Squash, winter	Varies with strain	65 to 110	65° O. to mid-summer	late summer to frost
Swiss Chard	¼ oz. sows 25-ft. row	55 to 65	55° O. (spring); resow late summer	early summer; late fall
Tomato, early	1/6 oz. yields 200+ plants	54 to 65	75° I.; transplant O. when warm	mid-summer
Tomato, main crop	1/6 oz. yields 200+ plants	65 to 85	75° I.; transplant O. when warm	mid-summer to frost
Turnip	⅛ oz. sows 30-ft. row	30 to 65	55° O. (spring); resow late summer	early summer; fall to late fall

*Temperatures refer to soil temperature. O. = outdoors, I. = indoors. L.K.F. date = last killing frost (average) date.

Index

Asparagus, 36–38
  choosing plants of, 37; delayed harvesting of, 36; discarding female plants of, 37; growing from seed, 37
Aubergine. *See* Eggplant

Beans, 39–47
  fast composting of, 43; fungicide-treated, 42, 45; nitrogen-fixing ability of, 39; selection recommendations, 41; sensitivity of plants and roots to fertilizer, 42; succession crops to, 42. *See also* Broad beans; Bush beans; Lima beans; Soy beans; Garbanzos
Beet, 48–51
  for fodder, 48; for greens, 48; Mono-germ strains, 48; temperature effects on, 48
Black-eyed peas, 127–128
  bacterial inoculum of seed, to aid nitrogen fixation, 127; bean pests attack, 128
Bolting, explanation of, 100
Bonemeal: as source of lime, 174
Boston lettuce. *See* Lettuce
Broad beans, 39–40
  cold tolerance of, 39; nitrogen-inoculum treated, 40; plants as compost, 39
Broccoli, 51–53
  and cabbage pests, 52; sprouting kinds recommended, 51; starting from seed, 51
Brussels sprouts, 54–56
  catch crop preceding, 54; hybrid sprouts' value, 55
Buckwheat family. *See* Rhubarb
Bush beans, 41–43
  in annual garden, 41; plants as compost, 42

Cabbage, 57–61
  alkalinity requirements of, 57; starting from seed, 58; table vs. commercial types, 57
Cabbage family. *See* Brussels sprouts; Kale; Kohlrabi

Cabbage pests: and rutabaga, 147–148
Calcuium: as carbonate, use of, 173; as lime, use of, 173–174; other sources of, 173
Cantaloupe. *See* Muskmelon
Captan: as fungicide for treated seed, 42–43, 45
Cardoons, 150
Carpetweed family. *See* New Zealand spinach
Carrot, 62–64
Carrot family. *See* Carrot; Celeriac; Celery; Parsley; Parsnip
Cauliflower, 65–67
  blanching, 66; cabbage pests attack, 66; colored forms of, 66; starting from seed indoors, 65
Cayenne peppers. *See* Peppers
Celeriac, 67
  celery diseases and pests attack, 67
Celery, 68–70
  blanching of, 68, 69, 70; early soil preparation, 68; starting seed indoors, 69
Celery cabbage. *See* Chinese cabbage
Celery root. *See* Celeriac
Celtuce, 71
Chard, 72
  beet pests attack, 72
Chick-peas. *See* Garbanzos
Chicory, 73–75
Chinese cabbage, 76–77
  direct sowing, 76; starting seed in flats, 76
Chinese lettuce, 71
Chlorosis, 173
Composite family. *See* Celtuce; Chicory; Dandelion; Lettuce; Salsify
Compost, 176–179
  defined, 176; for mulches, 177; shredding of, to kill pests, 177; sources of, 78, 176, 177, 178; sterilization of, 177
Container gardening, 180–184
  container insulation, 181; container selection, 180–181; fertilizing, 184; plants for, 182–184;

soil mixtures and preparation
for, 180–181
Copperas: for iron deficiency, 173
Corn, 79–81
earworms attack tomatoes, 164;
pollination, importance of,
78–79; rotary tiller use for, 78;
stalks as compost, 78; treated
seed for, 80
Cow peas, 127 –128
plants used for green manure,
129
Crenshaw. *See* Muskmelon
Cress, garden, 82
Crop rotation, 27 – 29
botanical relationships as guide
for, 29; and fertilizers, 28; soil
requirements as guide for, 29;
three-year chart for, 28
Cucumber family. *See* Cucumber;
Muskmelon; Pumpkin; Squash;
Watermelon
Cucumber, 83 – 85
Chinese and Japanese varieties
need trellis, 83; melon aphids
attack, 84; squash bugs attack,
84
Cultivation, summer, 26. *See also*
Cultivation and Management
section under individual vegetables

Dandelion, 86
Dolomitic limestone: as magnesium
source, 174
Dowfume: to sterilize compost, 177

Eggplant, 87 – 88
chill sensitivity of, 87; location
re: previous tomato and pepper
crops, 87; starting seed indoors,
87

Fava beans. *See* Broad beans
Fertilizer, 172 –175
application of, 42, 174 – 175;
and crop rotation, 28; fruiting
vegetables' needs, 174; functions of, 172; leafy vegetables'
needs, 174; liquid manure as,
175; N-P-K (Nitrogen-Phosphorus-Potassium) ratios of, 18,
172; organic formula for root
crops, 149; root vegetables'
needs, 174, side-dressing of,
175; trace elements in, 172 – 173.
See also individual vegetable
entries
French endive. *See* Chicory

Garbanzos, 89–90
bean pests attack, 90; location

re: previous year's crop, 89
Garden
city, 13, 30–33
home: vegetables recommended
for, 15
layout: Early spring garden,
31; late fall-early winter
garden, 33; space-demanding
crops, 16; summer garden,
32
location: drainage considerations, 13; root room in, 13;
sunlight considerations, 13, 14
maintenance: clearing of debris,
25; weeding, importance
of, 25
size: for first garden, 11–12;
per person requirements, 12
Garden peas, 124–126
location re: manured crop, 124;
treated seed for, 125
Garlic, 91
Goobers. *See* Peanuts
Goosefoot family. *See* Beets;
Chard; Spinach
Gourds. *See* Squash
Grass family. *See* Corn
Green manure: definition and use
of, 178–179; sources of, 39,
129, 178–179
Groundnuts. *See* Peanuts
Gumbo, 113–114

Honeydew, 106, 108. *See also*
Muskmelon
Horseradish, 92–93
in perennial border, 92; pests
attack other plants, 93
Hot peppers. *See* Peppers
Humus: described, 17

Insect Pests. *See* individual
vegetable listings
Iron: chelated, for chlorosis, 173;
deficiency, signs of, 173; plant
use of, 173; sources of, 173
Italian dandelion. *See* Chicory
Italian sprouting broccoli
(Calabrese). *See* Broccoli

Kale, 94–95
location re: previous season's
cabbage relatives, 94
Kohlrabi, 96–97
cabbage pests attack, 97;
starting from seed, 96

Leek, 98–99
blanching of, 98, 99; fresh
seed needed for, 98
Legume family. *See* Black-eyed
peas; Broad beans; Garbanzos;

Garden peas; Lima beans;
   Peanuts; Soy beans; Sugar peas
Lettuce, 100–104
   as a catch crop, 100; following
   heavily manured crop, 101;
   kinds of, 100; location re:
   previous lettuce crop, 103;
   space-saving method of sowing,
   102; starting indoors, 100
Lily family. *See* Garlic; Onion;
   Leek; Shallot
Lime, 173–174
   bonemeal as source of, 174;
   as calcium source, 173–174;
   explanation of, 173; as
   magnesium source, 174; use
   of, 173–174
Liquid manure: use of, 175

Madeira-vine family. *See* Malibar
   spinach
Magnesium: dolomitic limestone as
   source of, 174
Malibar spinach, 105
Mallow family. *See* Okra
Manure, 176–179
   distinguished from fertilizer,
   176, 177; horse, need for
   stacking, 176; liquid, use of,
   175; NPK content of, 177;
   sources of, 176; timing of
   application, 178; uses of,
   176–177
Manure, green. *See* Green manure
Melons. *See* Muskmelon;
   Watermelon
Mango melon. *See* Muskmelon
Morning glory family. *See* Sweet
   potato
Mulch: plastic, 26; use of, 171
Muskmelon, 106–108
   cucumber pests and diseases
   attack, 107; starting indoors,
   107
Mustard, 111–112
Mustard family. *See* Broccoli;
   Cabbage; Cauliflower; Chinese
   cabbage; Cress, garden;
   Horseradish; Mustard; Radish;
   Rutabaga; Turnip; Watercress

New Zealand Spinach, 154
   seed preparation of, 154
Nightshade family. *See* Eggplant;
   Pepper; Potato, Irish;
   Tomato
Nitrogen-Phosphorus-Potassium
   ratios: explained, 18, 172
NPK ratios: explained, 18, 172

Okra, 113–114
Onion, 115–117
   following heavily manured

crop, 115; kinds of, 115;
   starting from seed, 116; from
   plants or sets, 115
Organic fertilizer: strength
   compared to commercial
   fertilizer, 17
Oyster plant. *See* Salsify

Parsley, 118–119
   biennial nature of, 118
Parsnip, 120–121
   biennial nature of, 120; carrot
   pests and diseases attack, 121;
   locating on garden's side, 120;
   sown with radish to break
   soil, 121
Peanuts, 122–123
   corn pests attack, 123;
   recommended crop for
   children, 122
Peppergrass, 82
Peppers, 130–132
   corn and stem borers
   attack, 131; following heavily
   manured crop, 130; starting
   indoors, 130
Perennial bed: plants for, 145. *See
   also* Asparagus; Dandelion;
   Horseradish; Rhubarb;
   Watercress
Petunia: as host of tomato virus, 165
Planting: covering seed, 25; drill
   opening and irrigation,
   instructions for, 24; and
   location of fertilizers or
   manures, 25; timing of, 24,
   31, 32, 33. *See also* instructions
   under individual vegetable
   listings
Pokeweed: as host of tomato
   virus, 165
Pole beans. *See* Bush beans
Potato, Irish, 133–138
   "eyes," growth and preparation
   of, 134; germination time of,
   134; as host to tomato virus,
   165; virus transmitted by
   pests of, 137
Pumpkin, 141. *See also* Squash

Radish, 142–144
   to mark slow-germinating
   crops, 142–143; sown with
   carrots to break soil, 62; sown
   with parsnips to break soil, 121
Rhubarb, 145–146
   forcing early, 146; starting from
   seed, 145
Romaine. *See* Lettuce
Rotary tiller: with corn, 78; dangers
   of misuse, 23; and garden size,
   20; for weed control, 26
Rotation. *See* Crop rotation
Round potato. *See* Potato, Irish

Rutabaga, 147–148
  turnip and cabbage pests attack, 147–148

Salsify, 149–150
  biennial nature of, 149
Scallions, 116
Scorzonera. *See* Salsify
Sevin: hazards of using, 80, 88
Shallot, 151
Snap beans. *See* Bush beans
Soil cultivation: garden size for mechanical cultivation, 11; rotary tiller use in, 11. *See also* individual vegetable entries
Soil preparation: importance of, 17. *See also* individual vegetable entries
Soja beans. *See* Soy beans
Southern table peas. *See* Black-eyed peas
Soy beans: as succession crop to corn, 46; use of nitrogen-inoculum treated, 46
Spinach, 152–153
  neutral soil needed for, 152
Sprouting broccoli. *See* Broccoli
Squash, 155–158
  bush forms for small garden, 155; tin-can watering method, 155
Sugar peas, 129
Swede. *See* Rutabaga
Sweet peppers. *See* Peppers
Swiss chard. *See* Chard
Sweet potato, 139–140
  distinguished from yam, 139; starting your own plants, 139

Tobacco: as host to tomato virus, 165
Tomato, 159–168
  basket culture of, 9, 184; corn earworms attack, 164; crop localization for disease control, 166; damage from hormone-type weed killers, 166; deeply setting plants, 162; determinate growth of, 159–160, 162, 167, 168; direct-sown, 162; indeterminate growth of, 159, 162, 167, 168; Irish potato diseases attack, 136; pruning of hybrid, 162; pruning of indeterminate, 162, 163; Rototiller, row spacing for, 162; soil moisture for, 162, 163, 164; staking of, 164; starting seed indoors, 161; viruses hosted by Nightshade family relatives, 165; walnuts toxic to, 166
Topsoil
  ascertaining depth and porosity of, 19
  desirable qualities of, 18
  explanation of, 17
  loosening methods of: double-digging, 22; plowing, 19, 22; rotary tilling, 20, 23; spading, 19, 20, 21, 22
  organic fertilizing of, vs. commercial fertilizer, 17
Trace elements: in soil, 172–173
Turnip, 169–170
  as cold-frame crop, 169; greens, nutritional value of, 169; pests, and rutabaga, 147–148
Turnip-rooted celery. *See* Celeriac

Upland cress, 82

Vegetable marrow, 157. *See also* Squash

Watercress, 171
  perennial nature of, 171
Watermelon, 109–110
  for citron, 110
Weeding, importance of, 25
White potato. *See* Potato, Irish
Winter melon, 108. *See also* Muskmelon
Witloof chicory. *See* Chicory